Lament and Justice in African American History

Lament and Justice in African American History

By the Rivers of Babylon

Edited by

Timothy Fritz and Trisha Posey

LEXINGTON BOOKS
Lanham • Boulder • New York • London

Published by Lexington Books
An imprint of The Rowman & Littlefield Publishing Group, Inc.
4501 Forbes Boulevard, Suite 200, Lanham, Maryland 20706
www.rowman.com

86-90 Paul Street, London EC2A 4NE

Copyright © 2023 by The Rowman & Littlefield Publishing Group, Inc.

All rights reserved. No part of this book may be reproduced in any form or by any electronic or mechanical means, including information storage and retrieval systems, without written permission from the publisher, except by a reviewer who may quote passages in a review.

British Library Cataloguing in Publication Information Available

Library of Congress Cataloging-in-Publication Data Available

ISBN 9781666923124 (cloth : alk. paper) | ISBN 9781666923131 (epub)

∞™ The paper used in this publication meets the minimum requirements of American National Standard for Information Sciences—Permanence of Paper for Printed Library Materials, ANSI/NISO Z39.48-1992.

Dedication

To those who endured in faith, you are not forgotten.

Contents

Foreword ix
   Jemar Tisby

Introduction xi
   Timothy Fritz

PART I: LAMENT AND HISTORICAL PRACTICE 1

Chapter One: Nobody Knows the Trouble I've Seen: Black Lament in the Stories Untold 3
   Alicia K. Jackson

Chapter Two: Frederick Douglass's Fourth of July Speech, Lament, and Historical Memory 13
   Trisha Posey

Chapter Three: The Planet and the Pageant: John Mitchell Jr.'s Lament and W. B. Cridlin's Celebration in Richmond, Virginia, May 1922 25
   Peter Slade

Chapter Four: "I'm tired of funerals. I'm tired of it! We've got to stand up!": Collective Lament, Collective Anger and Collective Action in the Civil Rights Struggle 45
   Ansley Quiros

Chapter Five: "A Tribute in Tears and a Thrust for Freedom": Medgar Evers and the Politics of Lament 61
   Patrick L. Connelly

PART II: LAMENT AND HISTORICAL PEDAGOGY   73

Chapter Six: The Psalms and the Historical Pedagogy of Lament   75
Timothy Fritz

Chapter Seven: Teaching History in Mississippi: Lament as Pedagogy in an Era of Suffering, 2008–2022   87
Otis W. Pickett

Chapter Eight: A Pedagogy of Healing   101
Karen Johnson

Chapter Nine: A Mourning March: Learning Lament in the Classroom of the City   117
Gregory R. Perry

Index   129

About the Contributors   133

Foreword

Jemar Tisby

I only watched the video of George Floyd once. Just a few seconds of the visual is all I needed to see, and one time all the way through was all my heart could take. For a lot of people, that video, with its clear and casual brutality, served as a catalyst for antiracist action. In 2020, outrage over Floyd's killing—along with murders of Ahmaud Arbery and Breanna Taylor—helped move people from passivity to focus. They read books, watched documentaries, marched in the streets, and challenged their faith communities to take bolder stands for racial justice.

Yet in all that activity we seemed to move quickly on from grief to more "productive" endeavors. With so much racism to take on, grief seems like an indulgent emotion. Weeping, poring over memories, letting the pain wash over you—how does that change anything?

And yet grieve we must.

In his second letter to the church in Corinth, the Apostle Paul speaks of a necessary kind of grief—a grief that leads to transformation. In fact, he was glad they grieved. " I rejoice, not because you were grieved, but because you were grieved into repenting" (2 Corinthians 7:9). When we grieve, we open our hearts to be pierced by the agony of others. We learn, in the most sobering of ways, what it means to love our neighbors as ourselves. The pain of grieving is the pathway to solidarity with the suffering.

Another way of describing grief is to talk about lament. Lament is the gut-level reaction to a world that is not as it should be. Lament is the existential reminder that our bodies, minds, and souls were created for harmony and not the discordant cacophony of oppression. Lament calls us back to the reality that our creation is supernatural, and we are all meant for flourishing.

Lament and Justice in African-American History is a volume that illustrates a fact we'd sometimes rather ignore. On the journey toward justice lament is our constant companion. Lament is not something we can skip over on the way to justice, it is part of the path of justice itself. Weeping and working operate in a symbiotic relationship that keep us humble toward others and hungry for righteousness.

The stories contained in this book show us how the intense injustice of racism is the cause for justifiable lamentation among people of African descent and their allies. The authors in this book show us that history is rife with lament and that we dare not deny or downplay its presence. These true stories show us that racism is not a disembodied ideology, rather it comes with tangible actions that separate mothers from children, sever limbs from bodies, and force human beings to stand with tears in their eyes as they see the wicked prosper.

As a nation, the United States has experienced military, economic, and cultural dominance. We don't really know how to lose well. Instead we engage in myth-making and concealment. This is true even in the church. Christians have been some of the worse perpetrators of racism, yet so many individuals, churches, and denominations refuse to take any meaningful steps at repair. Perhaps part of this hesitancy arises from the failure to practice lament. It is indicative of our reticence to give up the triumphalist narratives with which we've inebriated ourselves.

Yet other Christians, particularly Black Christians, have been well-acquainted with the anguish of racism. We have been forced to dwell with disappointment in our nation and with our fellow spiritual brothers and sisters. You can hear it in the Negro spirituals sung by enslaved women and men sweltering under a hot sun. You can hear it our preachers who probe the Bible to make meaning of senseless suffering. You can measure it in our heightened blood pressure and mortality rates. Black Christians have much to teach this country about lament.

This book is your introduction to some of the lessons of lament and justice. Let these truth-tellers guide you deeper into the annals of our national sins and tarry with terribleness of slavery, segregation, and the many manifestations of white supremacy. These data are not pleasant, but they are indispensable for creating "tough minds" that shrewdly pursue racial justice and "tender hearts" that keep us warm and compassionate toward others. Lament is not a distraction from justice, it is the action that matures us into the kind of people who do justice well.

Introduction

Timothy Fritz

Memory is one of the bedrocks of community. Others' understanding informs relations between groups of people of their stories. Yet, as the essays in the following pages show, modern day Americans face challenges in understanding the painful parts of our own stories, to say nothing of the divergent experiences of others with whom we share a community. The authors of this volume point to the value of the biblical practice of lament as essential to understanding our neighbors and strengthening community. The Christian process of lament, examined here as expressing grief, sorrow, confusion, or dissatisfaction with God, is a painful undertaking often relegated to private spaces in American culture. As the books of Lamentations and Psalms show, lament opens a public conversation to critically assess humanity's responsibility to each other and the Christian's understanding of God's promises to humanity. Out of this often angry and frustrated practice springs a better appreciation of life, if not always a reprieve from the troubling circumstance. Through lament's defined stages of anguish at present circumstances moving towards a request for diving intervention based on biblical promises, engaging in the uniquely Christian practice of lament as a reflective conversation with God systematically moves us beyond a simple desire for a happy ending to our struggles. Instead, it illuminates the value of the mundane and the significance of suffering.

Examining the history of the African American responses to displacement, enslavement, and racial violence in the United States demonstrates the power of lament in regenerating communities in the face of hard times, in many ways echoing the experiences of biblical Hebrew practices of lament in exile. Expressions of this process are visible throughout American culture, from the negro spirituals to blues music which became part of mainstream twentieth century entertainment. Certainly, traumatic events do not define the experiences of people of color in this country, but the response of these communities to systematic oppression gestures to the potential power of communal lament. One cannot simply disregard adverse historical circumstances with generational impact. History is important not for its exceptions but for the accurate representation of the human experience.

By the Rivers of Babylon explores the history of various expressions of the theology of lament in the African American community and situates this practice in the broader currents of American history in a way that provides a roadmap for present day discussion. In exploring how everyone can engage with a painful past not necessarily their own, it also comments on the promise of lament as a method of understanding humanity in the university classroom and the responsibility of universities to promote cultural awareness in their communities. Together, lament as historical practice encourages a complete historiographical account of the American story, inspiring a better historical memory that accounts for the full diversity of experiences. Moreover, when universities employ this model in neighborhood and classroom discussions, they can create a culturally literate populace who critically examine and actively search for missing historical voices in pursuit of a complete community understanding of both triumph and sorrow with an eye towards reconciliation.

PART I

Lament and Historical Practice

Chapter One

Nobody Knows the Trouble I've Seen

Black Lament in the Stories Untold

Alicia K. Jackson

Leroy Jones loved to tell stories. He was to his children and grandchildren not only a storyteller, but the repository of his family's history. Born in 1916, Leroy Jones stood 5'7 with a lean frame and skin that was both smooth and textured from years of tilling the soil of his 60-acre farm in southwest Georgia. After the death of his parents, he and his brother were raised by his maternal grandparents who were both born just as the promise of Reconstruction drew to a close in early 1870s Georgia. Countless uncles, aunts, and cousins surrounded him in Georgia as did stories told by his grandparents, Maw and Paw, and by his great grandfather who had been enslaved and had gained his emancipation only to become blind soon after. There was also Grandma Afri who had a direct connection to Africa, a place so close and yet so unfamiliar to him, and yet Leroy Jones maintained a similarly direct connection through his storytelling and his experience of traditions found throughout continental Africa. As such, he highlights the importance of the Black oral tradition as an expression of wisdom and lament in the African American community.

By telling, retelling, and preserving of stories, Leroy Jones maintained a connection to traditions found throughout continental Africa such as the place of the community griot or the practice of bringing children in on important communal events with the expectation that they sit quietly or leave. This practice encouraged children to listen to elders and appreciate the privilege of being invited into adult spaces. Consequently, they formed strong bonds with older members of their communities, who were possessors of great wisdom, and they learned to honor elders of their community which in turn discouraged any notions of old age as a detriment.[1] In addition, older community members, who were often grandparents, cared for younger children while parents were working, and this built bonds with elders and infused children with a strong sense of self-esteem.[2]

These elders were "riveting storytellers" to their young audiences and interpreters of the past as experienced in the reality of the present, and Leroy Jones was virtually an apprentice as he learned the art of storytelling from his elders.[3] As an adult with a family of his own, the Georgia tobacco farmer would sit on his porch many a nights, telling the stories he had heard in the cool evenings with his elders. With no central air, the porch and the cool breezes of the evening provided relief from the thick, dense Georgia heat and the gnats that demanded constant attention during the heat of the day. Although the family owned a radio and television, the storytelling experience was special and on occasion, was punctuated with a hymn or two as he sang bass and his family sang their parts in harmony. The tenuous experiences of a formerly enslaved person often meant the frequent experience of family separation, and the sharing of stories allowed enslaved people who were brought together either out of necessity or ancestry to bond together under a shared communal experience. Within the sharing of tales and songs was a sacred quality, possibly a "connecting" of one generation to another, and Black men and women like Leroy Jones relied on oral traditions to preserve both slave and family stories. His childhood was centered on his sense of community and he was imbued with generations of knowledge through the bequeathing of stories from slavery and emancipation. This chapter explores stories from the oral Black tradition as expressions of wisdom and lament and the impact that the failure to share these stories has had on African Americans.

Brer Rabbit was cunning, meek, greedy, and sometimes deceitful depending on the situation, and he is one of many gifts given to Leroy Jones and rooted in the storytelling of Black communities. As noted by scholars, stories of wizened animals told by enslaved African Americans flowed directly from African culture with recognizable counterparts. The animals of Africa were replaced by animals referred to as "Brer," which was a shortened version of "Brother," and Brer Rabbit is set in a contest with Brer Fox, Brer Dawg, and Brer Bear. Brer Rabbit finds a counterpart in the hare depicted in stories from Angola and parts of Nigeria. In fact, the tortoise and the spider from Nigeria, Ghana, and Liberia are deeply rooted in regions where enslaved Africans originated, and many of Brer rabbit's predicaments mirror the Yoruba tortoise and Anansi, the spider, who is also a trickster. In African stories, confrontations explode between the physically stronger lion, leopard, or elephant, and the weaker hare or spider in the same way as they do between Brer Bear, Brer Fox, and the weaker yet cunning Brer Rabbit.

The merging of African and American figures in storytelling demonstrated the consolidation of distinctive African culture and the realities of Black life in America. Masters, who were distrustful of slave culture, restricted dance and music among slaves, but stories told by slaves were allowed because they seemed to be harmless entertainment. These stories gained national prominence in the United States outside the Black community with the publication of Joel Chandler Harris's collection of folktales in the late nineteenth century. A white Georgian, Harris hoped to promote the idea of a passive Black population as part of his championing the New South. For whites, these tales served as harmless children's stories from Black communities, and their redacting among white audiences continued well into the twentieth century, most notably with the release of the 1946 Walt Disney film, *Song of the South*.

Although not as prominent outside of the Black community as were the Brer Rabbit stories, John the Conqueror, who was an enslaved trickster, represented the slave who was willing to try and outsmart the "marster." John's tales were based on everyday occurrences and focused on his attempts to outsmart "marster," but he frequently was himself tricked instead of being the trickster. The tales were shared throughout the Black communities often with little variation in basic story lines, and their similarities reinforced their universality and the importance of the oral tradition in the slave community. They reveal the purity and reliability of slave folklore that used oral culture as both a means of passing along important history and morality.[4] Moreover, for enslaved people, these stories served as psychological devices that supported mental health, involving little physical threat, and providing recreation.[5] Slave stories in the United States "were [not] necessarily African," but a number of aspects of the tales had similar themes and were "often infused with [a] direct moral message."[6] The stories told represented the resilience of African Americans who through the oral tradition bound their communities together in both the telling and experience of their shared history.

The authenticity and successful delivery of these stories often depended on the relationship between the storytellers and their hearers. According to historian Lawrence Levine, oral tradition served as the "slave version of history, [and] like all slave tales were enhanced by the manner of their delivery."[7] This required a dynamic connection between the deliverers and their hearers' experience as well as the engagement of all of their senses. It also meant that the community of hearers provided immediate response, which was a direct link to the call and response characteristically experienced in the Black oral tradition.

The rich oral tradition extends not only into family histories and community stories, but also into traditions found in African-American preaching. Hoping to replace traditional African beliefs, some slave owners allowed for the proselytizing of Christianity among enslaved people but restricted preaching and teaching to either white ministers or Black ministers closely supervised by White leaders. However, African-American preachers implicitly challenged this arrangement by creating a distinct religious community known as "brush arbors" which served as the foundation of much of the Black Church. Remnants of the preaching originating in brush arbors are no more apparent than in James Weldon Johnson's *God's Trombones*, which is a compilation of what he described as "rather vague memories of sermons" beginning with creation and culminating with judgment day.[8]

The folk sermon "Go Down Moses" from Johnson's collection tells the story of Moses who, when called by God at the burning bush, replies, "I'm Slow of Tongue," to which God responds, "I will be thy mouth and I will be thy tongue." When Moses does go down to speak to Pharaoh and is refused, the preacher responds, "Poor Old Pharaoh, He knows all the knowledge of Egypt . . . He never knew, The one and the living God."[9] The message of perseverance against the odds is clear in the sermon as Moses is ill-equipped to challenge the leader of a powerful nation like Egypt, but his success is built upon a more powerful, unseen source. Eventually Pharaoh lets the Israelites go but has a change of mind culminating in the miraculous parting of the Red Sea by God as the Israelites make their escape. Midway through their crossing, Pharoah and his army drown when the waters return. The folk sermon ends with the pointed reminder, "All you sons of Pharaoh. Who do you think can hold God's people? When the Lord God himself has said, Let my people go?"[10] The ending line serves as a warning for those who are holding God's people in bondage. They too face the possibility of a disastrous ending like that of Pharaoh.

The sermon also reminded Black hearers of their former condition as slaves and their struggle against the injustice experienced during the post-emancipation period. Known as the nadir of race relations, the late nineteenth and early twentieth century was rife with efforts to return African Americans to a condition of servitude that culminated in racial violence that targeted their communities and fueled the adoption of Jim Crow laws. "Go Down Moses" provided a connection to the past and a reminder of God's ultimate control. Moreover, the folk sermon created a direct connection between the experience of the Black church and that of the Israelites of the Old Testament who suffered under the brutal slavery of the Egyptian Pharaoh who lets them go and then regrets his decision. Similarly, Black Americans were freed through the Emancipation Proclamation but found themselves "re-enslaved" with the rise and implementation of Jim Crow. The ending line of the sermon is a reminder of God's control and his ultimate authority that could lead to a demise similar to Pharaoh.

In Johnson's folk sermon, "The Crucifixion" Jesus is described as "gentle" and "burdened" by his impending brutal death and the betrayal of his "black hearted" disciple, Judas, before being taken before Pilate, the Roman governor. The insult and brutality escalates over the course of the sermon as Johnson writes, "And they beat my loving Jesus, They spit on my precious Jesus . . . They put a crown of thorns upon his head, And they mocked my sweet King Jesus." Johnson then connects the crucifixion directly to the Black experience by writing, "And then they laid hold on Simon, Black Simon, yes, black Simon; They put the cross on Simon, And Simon bore the cross." The sermon ends with Jesus' Mother, Mary, watching His death: "Mary, Weeping Mary, Sees her poor little Jesus on the cross. Mary, Weeping Mary, Sees her sweet, baby Jesus on the cruel cross, Hanging between two thieves."[11]

For African Americans the injustice of Jesus's crucifixion is furthered by the reality of his innocence of any wrongdoing and by Simon who is forced to bear the cross alongside Jesus. Lastly, the injustice is punctuated by Mary, his mother, watching as her son is put to death in such brutality. For enslaved mothers, the story of the mistreatment of Jesus connected directly to their experience of watching children being sold away, abused, and beaten, with little recourse. Both "Go Down Moses" and "The Crucifixion" exemplify what Albert J. Raboteau describes as the experience of African American Christians who see themselves as "a chosen people, not because they were black, nor because they suffered, but because their history fit the pattern of salvation revealed to them in the Bible." As he writes, "They saw themselves in Christ, the suffering servant. Their lives modeled the paradoxes of the gospel: in weakness lies strength, in loss, gain, in death, life."[12]

As Levine explains, enslaved African Americans used both stories and sermons in ways that gave them "psychological release from the inhibitions of their society and their situation."[13] They were often an important part of, "the art of surviving and even triumphing in the face of a hostile environment."[14] Living in the reality of Jim Crow, oral folk culture provided an opportunity for Black people to laugh and rehearse tactics to challenge oppressive environments, power structures, and teach "their young the means they would have to adapt [and] to survive."[15]

Storytelling and the more sacred practice of sermonizing allowed Black people to testify to life's realities. They were tools of direct action that could be used as a way of challenging enslavement, and later, Jim Crow. Historian Kidada Williams explains that "Testifying about racial violence was a crucial factor in African Americans' individual recovery and their collective resistance to white supremacy because whenever victims related their experiences of this violence, they created witnesses to their trauma. Family members, friends, and neighbors were the first people that victims made bear witness to suffering they endured or witnessed."[16] Before Emancipation, only a handful of free Black men and women had the freedom to discuss their history and experience in a public forum. Consequently, when the promise of Reconstruction arrived, the formerly enslaved extended the telling of their stories from Black communities to a broader audience in white communities, albeit on their terms. Reconstruction was the first time in American History that Black voices testified to power. Formerly enslaved Black people testified to the Executive branch of government via the Freedmen's Bureau, and also to the Legislative branch via Congressional Committees. Testimonies to the impact of racial violence and other injustices heaped upon their families and communities developed into the Progressive movement which stretched well into the twentieth century.[17] These testimonials were built upon a tradition of sharing hard truths, through stories and sermons, first within the African American community.

Efforts to preserve the life stories of formerly enslaved people occurred in the 1930s as the Works Progress Administration (WPA) and Black institutions like Fisk began collecting interviews from formerly enslaved Americans. The stories collected presented a more complicated America by challenging prevalent versions of American history which tended to be "triumphalistic, smug, or celebratory" but failed to present the full truth of all Americans adequately. In fact, the lives of Black Americans spoke of a "continual awareness that racial inequity has been woven into the fabric of our society from the start and is still very much a part of its social and economic pattern."[18] As Albert J. Robeatu notes from his study of African American religion, "the voices I heard spoke, in the main, with righteous anger and prophetic certainty about the destruction awaiting this nation unless it repented of the sin of racism. Their God was a God of justice they asserted, the Lord of history, who intervened in human affairs to cast down the mighty and uplift the lowly"[19] It was justice not only meted out in the world to come but also in the here and now.

According to psychologist Judith Herman, "The knowledge of horrible events periodically intrudes into public awareness but is rarely retained. Denial, repression, and dissociation operate on a social as well as individual level." What happens when the oral tradition dies and testifying so long part of the Black experience in America ends? The danger in being "cut off" from the knowledge of past trauma limits the ability to understand current realities and demands a rediscovery of history in order to understand the impact of "psychological trauma" that reaches from the past to the present.[20] Herman describes how the activism of the women's liberation movement in the 1970s was spurred on by women publicly discussing the violence they experienced. Later when she shared her work with female patients who also experienced sexual and domestic violence, women from all over the country shared similar stories as they saw the veil of silence removed. According to Herman, the telling of stories, and especially traumatic events, is a "precondition for the restitution of a sense of a meaningful world," and not only serves as "public acknowledgement of the traumatic event" but also encourages "some form of community action."[21]

Moreover, the disconnect from these oral traditions for Black Americans is also a break away from the traditions of African culture. Vital to the grasp and conception of African culture is, according to Raboteau, the "personalized world of traditional African religion [where] the self is conceived as relational. Each person is constituted by a web of interpersonal relationships." As he explains, "Our health, our fortunes, our very lives depend upon the state of our relationships with others, including those who have gone before, our ancestors, who continue to figure prominently in the progress of our lives. By contrast, the tendency of American culture to overemphasize the individualized self empties life of the communal presence that gives depth and background to our existence."[22] Pointedly, in traditional African religion, the focus on the individual self is "witchcraft, pure and simple."[23]

In the role of the community storyteller and historian, the griot from Africa served as a repository to remember and instruct future generations. Similar roles were part of many families as grandparents and elder family members passed on vital history and oral culture. When folk culture is no longer preserved through story-telling or through the more sacred practice of traditional Black preaching, deadly silences are created. According to Michel-Rolph Trouillot, "We all need histories that no history book can tell . . . They are in the lessons we learn at home, in poetry and childhood games, in what is left of history when we close the history books with their verifiable facts."[24] When the transmission ends, the story told is based purely on what has already been written or shared by historians who have historically overlooked folk culture's stories and experiences as unviable historical sources. Notably, according to an April 14, 2022 Pew Research report, "Black adults under 30 (50%) are less likely than those 65 and older (64%) to say their ancestors were enslaved. In fact, 40% of Black adults under 30 say that they are not sure whether their ancestors were enslaved. Black adults in the youngest age group (59%) are less likely than the oldest (87%) to have spoken to their relatives about family history or to have used a mail-in DNA service to learn about their ancestors (11% vs. 21%)."[25] The Pew results clearly indicate that younger Black Americans have less connection with relatives in understanding their family histories and the Black experience in America.

A disconnect with the past seems more pronounced as African Americans try to make sense of the uptick in racial violence and hostility in the early twenty-first century as typified by a number of incidents including the shooting at a Black Church and at a supermarket frequented predominantly by African Americans, the contamination of drinking water in Black neighborhoods, the frequent shooting of unarmed Black men, women and children, and the growth of mass incarceration. The break in connection to the rich oral culture of the past means a disconnect from stories and truths that have shaped African Americans and their understanding of the world around them for centuries. Instead, a chasm is created, wisdom is forgotten, history is erased, and ancestors disappear. The final result is a break with the traditions that have long shaped the Black experience in America.

Without the creation, assembling, and retrieval of their own oral culture the consequence for African Americans is dire. If the only stories being told are those that perceive Black culture as a source of problems or victimization with little to no agency, then there is no counter narrative. In the early twenty first century, a common narrative shared in Black communities is known as "the talk." Typically given by parents, "the talk" focuses on ways Black men and women should interact with law enforcement to avoid dire consequences including death. Unfortunately, this discussion and its story provide little opportunity for African Americans to narratively shape outcomes or transmit morality. Instead, the crux of this story is built upon an overarching fear of the unknown, the presumption of helplessness, and an expectation of a negative outcome.

To some, Black oral traditions that for centuries encompassed Black life may serve as an exercise of nostalgia, and yet, its demise creates a disconnect from the stories that have tied millions of people together despite the horrors of the Trans-Atlantic slave trade and American chattel slavery. The stories that Black parents have shared with their children and grandchildren, and the narrative sermons that Black preachers have shared with their congregations and communities, perhaps will one day flow again from one generation to the other like borrowed breath.[26]

BIBLIOGRAPHY

Adoff, Arnold, ed. *The Poetry of Black America: Anthology of the 20th Century.* New York: Harper Collins, 1973.

Blassingame, John. *The Slave Community: Plantation Life in the Antebellum South.* New York: University of Oxford Press, 1979.

Cox, Kiana and Christine Tamir. "Race Is Central to Identity for Black Americans and Affects How They Connect With Each Other." Pew Research Center. https://www.pewresearch.org/race-ethnicity/2022/04/14/race-is-central-to-identity-for-black-americans-and-affects-how-they-connect-with-each-other/.

Dorson, Richard. *American Negro Folktale.* Mineola, New York: Dover, 1967.

Herman, Judith. *Trauma and Recovery: The Aftermath of Violence form Domestic Abuse to Political Terror.* New York: Basic Books, 2015.

Johnson, James Weldon. *God's Trombones: Seven Negro Sermons in Verse.* New York: Viking Press, 1927.

Khapoya, Vincent B. *The African Experience: An Introduction*, 2nd ed. Upper Saddle River, New Jersey: Prentice Hall, 1998.

Levine, Lawrence. *Black Culture and Black Consciousness: Afro American Folk Thought from Slavery to Freedom*, 30th anniversary ed. Oxford: Oxford University Press, 2007.

Raboteau, Albert J., *A Fire in the Bones: Reflections on African American Religious History*. Boston: Beacon Press, 1995.

Trouillot, Michel-Rolph. *Silencing the Past: Power and the Production of History*. Boston: Beacon Press, 2015.

Williams, Kidada E. *They Left Great Marks on Me: African American Testimonies of Racial Violence from Emancipation to World War I*. New York: New York University Press, 2012.

NOTES

1. Vincent B. Khapoya, *The African Experience: An Introduction*, 2nd ed. (Upper Saddle River, New Jersey: Prentice Hall, 1998), 41–42.
2. Khapoya, *The African Experience*, 52.
3. Khapoya, *The African Experience*, 41–42, 52.
4. Leroy Jones's John the Conqueror story, "Massa goes on a Trip" is a virtual match to a similar John the Conqueror story found in Richard Dorson's *American Negro Folktales* titled "Old Marster Takes a Trip" (Mineola, New York: Dover, 1967), 222.
5. John Blassingame, *The Slave Community: Plantation Life in the Antebellum South*, (New York: University of Oxford Press, 1979), 129.
6. Lawrence Levine, *Black Culture and Black Consciousness: Afro American Folk Thought from Slavery to Freedom*, 30th anniversary ed. (Oxford: Oxford University Press, 2007), 82, 90.
7. Levine, *Black Culture and Black Consciousness*, 88.
8. James Weldon Johnson, *God's Trombones: Seven Negro Sermons in Verse* (New York: Viking Press, 1927), 5, accessed July 31, 2022, https://docsouth.unc.edu/southlit/johnson/johnson.html.
9. Johnson, *God's Trombones*, 47.
10. Johnson, *God's Trombones*, 52, 1.
11. Johnson, *God's Trombones*, 39–42.
12. Albert J Raboteau, *A Fire in the Bones: Reflections on African American Religious History* (Boston: Beacon Press, 1995), 192.
13. Levine, *Black Culture and Black Consciousness*, 102.
14. Levine, *Black Culture and Black Consciousness*, 115.
15. Levine, *Black Culture and Black Consciousness*, 125.
16. Kidada E. Williams, *They Left Great Marks on Me: African American Testimonies of Racial Violence from Emancipation to World War I* (New York: New York University Press, 2012), 5.
17. Williams, *They Left Great Marks on Me*, 10.

18. Raboteau, *A Fire in the Bones*, 186.

19. Raboteau, *A Fire in the Bones*, 187.

20. Judith Herman, *Trauma and Recovery: The Aftermath of Violence form Domestic Abuse to Political Terror* (New York: Basic Books, 2015), 2.

21. Judith Herman, *Trauma and Recovery*, 70.

22. Raboteau, *A Fire in the Bones,* 190–191.

23. Raboteau, *A Fire in the Bones*, 191.

24. Michel-Rolph Trouillot, *Silencing the Past: Power and the Production of History* (Boston: Beacon Press, 2015), 26, 71–72.

25. Kiana Cox and Christine Tamir, "Race Is Central to Identity for Black Americans and Affects How They Connect With Each Other," Pew Research Center, https://www.pewresearch.org/race-ethnicity/2022/04/14/race-is-central-to-identity-for-black-americans-and-affects-how-they-connect-with-each-other/.

26. Reference taken from A.B. Spelman, "When Black People Are," *The Poetry of Black America: Anthology of the 20th Century*, ed. Arnold Adoff (New York: Harper Collins, 1973), 284–85.

Chapter Two

Frederick Douglass's Fourth of July Speech, Lament, and Historical Memory

Trisha Posey

In recent years, white Americans have had to wrestle with the realities of racial injustice and they are turning to history to understand the ways the past has shaped modern racial reality. Many African American leaders have argued for decades that a proper understanding of American history ought to directly address the many ways racial injustice has shaped the American past and present. In 1963, the year of the hundredth anniversary of the Emancipation Proclamation, James Baldwin wrote a public letter to his nephew. In this letter Baldwin sought to describe the dangerous world his nephew was inheriting. It was a world that destroyed black bodies and the black spirit, a world that was designed for black death. "This innocent country set you down in a ghetto in which, in fact, it intended you should perish," Baldwin wrote.[1] The use of the descriptor "innocent" was, of course, no accident here. Indeed, Baldwin used the word several times in his letter to emphasize the dangerous naivety of whites who blindly subscribed to the myth of American goodness while perpetuating systems of oppression that harmed Black women and men. Baldwin described white Americans as "still trapped in a history which they do not understand." Until they understand it, Baldwin told his nephew, "they cannot be released from it."[2] For Baldwin, Black emancipation was tied to the deliverance of whites from their false understandings of American history.

In response to African American leaders like Baldwin, many white Americans have begun to turn to African American leaders of the past for wisdom and insight on the important issue of racial injustice. Few historical leaders are more fitted to speak to present realities of racial injustice than

Frederick Douglass, the nineteenth-century abolitionist. One particular popularization of Douglass over the past few years has been the posting and re-posting of his 1852 Fourth of July speech to the Rochester Anti-Slavery Society. With his soaring rhetoric, Douglass delivered in this speech one of the most forceful condemnations of the evils of slavery on one of the most sacred days in American culture.

In his Fourth of July speech Douglass also asked his audience to consider the connections between history, memory, lament, and hope and challenged them to reconsider a celebrated past through the lens of the sufferer. In doing so, he attacked one of the most sacred cows of American history, the American founding, and forced his listeners to wonder how their malformed memory contributed to the ongoing suffering of African Americans. He called upon his audience to engage in lament and then to respond to that lament with a turn toward justice. Douglass, in this way, spoke not only as a former enslaved man, but as a historian, pastor, and theologian all at once. In bringing together history and theology Douglass challenged not only his contemporary audience, but also modern Americans, to consider the role of lament in our engagement with the past.

Frederick Douglass was born in 1818 on the Eastern Shore of Maryland. The son of an enslaved African American woman and a free white man (probably his master), Douglass spent his early years as an enslaved person moving between the rural agricultural setting of the Eastern Shore and the urban world of Baltimore. Douglass fled slavery in 1838 and settled in New Bedford and then Lynn, Massachusetts. While in Massachusetts, he became a licensed preacher and met leading abolitionists, including William Lloyd Garrison. Garrison recruited Douglass to speak on the anti-slavery circuit, and Douglass became one of the most sought-after abolitionist speakers in New England. In 1845 Douglass published *Narrative of the Life of Frederick Douglass*, a text that was developed and refined through the hundreds of abolitionist speeches that he had given. It became a best-seller and propelled Douglass to international fame. Douglass went to Ireland and Great Britain to spread his abolitionist message, and while abroad he experienced what can only be called a new birth in his understanding of American racial dynamics.

Indeed, upon returning to New England in 1847, Douglass began the process of breaking away from those white supporters who had previously sought to shape the narrative he told about his own life. He started his own abolitionist newspaper, broke from Garrison, and struck out on his own as a speaker and publisher. It was in this context, one in which he was starting to openly criticize not just white southern slave-holders, but white northern abolitionists as well, that Douglass was invited to give what became his most famous speech.

In 1852 the ladies of the Rochester Anti-Slavery Society invited Douglass to give their annual Fourth of July speech. Fourth of July speeches had become annual events in American towns and cities and were moments to celebrate the founding principles of liberty and freedom. At these celebrations, special attention was paid to the founding documents of America's civil religion, the Constitution and the Declaration of Independence. Douglass, who lived in Rochester at the time, had close ties to the society. His good friend Julia Griffiths was secretary of the society and earlier in the year the women of the society had raised $233 to support Douglass's abolitionist newspaper. It is difficult to know what the Rochester Anti-Slavery Society was expecting from Douglass that day. Douglass had come out as a strong proponent of the idea that the Constitution was, in fact, an anti-slavery document. Perhaps the expectation was that Douglass was going to talk about this revered text and call his audience to remember its ideals. Whatever the society was expecting, what the five to six hundred people who were in the audience received was one of the harshest critiques of American society and white American northerners to date. Douglass's audience could not have left that space feeling confident or proud of themselves; indeed, the entire purpose of the speech was to call self-assured white northerners out of their slumber to a new, more truthful understanding of the American past they had so confidently claimed as one of triumph and progress.

Douglass spent the first third of his speech laying out a narrative of American history in a manner with which his audience would have been very familiar. Linking his audience's Christian faith to their national celebration, Douglass started by saying, "This, for the purpose of this celebration, is the 4th of July. It is the birthday of your National Independence, and of your political freedom. This, to you, is what the Passover was to the emancipated people of God."[3] Following this baptizing of the American Revolution with the rhetoric of Judeo-Christian faith, Douglass then laid out the story of the nation's independence. Over and over again, Douglass highlighted the ideas that drove the founders to their break from England. "Under the inspiration of glorious patriotism, and with a sublime faith in the great principles of justice and freedom, lay deep the corner-stone of the national superstructure, which has risen and still rises in grandeur around you,"[4] Douglass noted in the climax of his story of American progress.

It is probable that Douglass's audience noted his use of the words "you" and "your" repeatedly in this early part of his speech. Douglass placed the narrative outside himself in his telling of the American past. The story he was telling was glorious, but it was not his. If, for some reason, Douglass's audience failed to pick up on this nuance in his speech, they would have been jarred at one key moment. Having laid out his narrative of the American Revolution, tying together religious ideologies with first principles for his

Christian audience, Douglass then turned the screw. Before presenting his alternative understanding of the founding for his audience, Douglass paused to ponder the meaning of historical remembrance. "My business," he noted, "if I have any here to-day, is with the present. The accepted time with God and his cause is the ever-living now. . . . We have to do with the past only as we can make it useful to the present and to the future."[5]

In speaking of the culture-shaping role of history and memory, Douglass as addressing a reality about the past that many historians have recognized—that the past is as much about myth building for present purposes as it is about understanding the lives and cultures of peoples who have come before us. Richard Hughes gives us a working definition of history as myth in his book *Myths America Lives By*: "[A] myth is a story that, whether true or false, helps us discern the meaning and purpose of our lives and, for that reason, speaks truth to those who embrace it."[6] Hughes is by no means the first historian to consider the nature and role of myths in American life. As far back as 1932 Carl Becker described history as "the artificial extension of social memory."[7] More recently, David Blight has spoken about the relationship between history and myth. "If history is shared and secular," Blight writes, "memory is often treated as a sacred set of absolute meanings and stories, possessed as the heritage or identity of a community."[8] It is precisely because myths play such a central role in identity that they are so difficult to address—their power is in their ability to give meaning to one's existence. Frederick Douglass understood this well. He grasped how the founding had become a mythological influence on white American culture and understood the power of historical memory to shape present realities. And for Douglass, the present reality was indeed grim. It was only after having established what he believed to be the purpose of historical memory that Douglass turned the moment of historical remembrance into one of lament.

"Fellow-citizens," he asked sardonically,

> pardon me, allow me to ask, why am I called upon to speak here today? What have I, or those I represent, to do with your national independence? Are the great principles of political freedom and of natural justice, embodied in that Declaration of Independence, extended to us? And am I, therefore, called upon to bring our humble offering to the national altar, and to confess the benefits and express devout gratitude for the blessings resulting from your independence to us?[9]

The answer, of course, was a mocking "no." He would not speak words of untruth for the sake of tickling his audience's ears. Instead, he argued that the Fourth of July was "vanity," "empty and heartless," "mockery," "bombast, fraud, deception, impiety, and hypocrisy" to those who were left out of the liberty and justice that was so openly boasted about during the "sham" of a holiday.[10]

In laying out his argument of hypocrisy against his audience and other white Americans, Douglass was simultaneously supporting the values for which the American Revolutionaries fought. One cannot be declared a hypocrite unless measured against a standard or principle they themselves have declared. Indeed, over and over again, Douglass pointed to the lamentable reality that what made the Fourth so galling to African Americans was that the truths that were being celebrated, the transcendent ideas of liberty, justice, humanity, law and religion, were principles to which enslaved persons themselves adhered, even while they were being denied their reality on a daily basis.

Douglass saved some of his harshest critique for the American church, which had largely been supportive or ambivalent about slavery. Calling on the words of Isaiah, Douglass declared that Americans' sham religion left them with, in his words, "HANDS . . . FULL OF BLOOD."[11] Even while Douglass called upon the church to repent, he simultaneously questioned its ability to do so. If the evidences of the evils of slavery had not been enough to convince them to change their ways, what *would*? Douglass protested, "At the very moment they [that is, white Christians] are thanking God for the enjoyment of civil and religious liberty, and for the right to worship God according to the dictates of their own consciences, they are utterly silent in respect to the law which robs religion of its chief significance." Douglass was referring here to The Fugitive Slave Law, which, he argued left religious organizations utterly impotent to show "benevolence, justice, love, and good will."[12] Any so-called Christian who followed the Fugitive Slave Law was putting the law of man before the law of God, and this, to Douglass, was the ultimate betrayal of Christian truth, making American Christianity "a hissing byword to a mocking earth."

These were harsh words for his white Christian audience, who surely received them with some trepidation. But Douglass did not leave it there. As with any good Jeremiad, the speech ended on a hopeful note. Douglass argued that a rediscovery of the Constitution, the rising forces of democracy and globalism, and an ascending Africa would pave the path toward the downfall of slavery. Notably, he did not mention the church playing a role in this new future.

At the time Douglass gave his speech, it was greeted with shouts and applause. It was widely distributed throughout the north; Douglass published the speech in his newspaper on July 9 and then it was reprinted as a pamphlet and added as an appendix to *My Bondage and My Freedom*, the second of his three autobiographies. But how do modern Americans receive this text?

If, as Douglass argues, "The accepted time with God and his cause is the ever-living now," how do Americans understand Douglass's speech in light of the challenge to tell the truth about the past, with all of its lamentable realities?

First, Douglass often reminded his audience that his understanding of American history was different than theirs because of his situational reality. "I shall see, this day, and its popular characteristics, from the slave's point of view," Douglass stated.[13] Douglass was not *choosing* to see the past differently, he stated that he was "compelled" to view history from a distinctly different perspective. He had no choice. He could see the beauty of the first principles preached by the founders, but he could also not help but see the other historical realities at play at the time of American Independence. The brutal scars of slavery were literally imprinted on the bodies of his mother and his grandmother, and all the other enslaved men and women who had been alive at the time of the founding. Douglass's plea to hear *his* story, from *his* perspective, is a plea that is still operative for American historians today. Historians must intentionally place before their audiences the narratives of those who, in the words of Ta-Nehisi Coates, have lived in a system that "dislodges brains, blocks airways, rips muscles, extracts organs, cracks bones, [and] breaks teeth."[14] Modern historians can learn from Douglass by understanding the complexities of human behavior and speaking the truth about those complexities in the stories they tell.

More fundamentally, Douglass teaches modern historians about the value of lament in the study of American history. Douglass's speech not only reimagined the American past, it followed a pattern of lament in response to that reimagining. Douglass's lament was deeply Christian in nature, rooted in the Biblical pattern of lament that would have been familiar both to him and his audience. His purpose, he stated, was to "take up the plaintive lament of a peeled and woe-smitten people!" Immediately following this stark statement of lament, Douglass launched into a recitation of Psalm 137: "By the rivers of Babylon, there we sat down. Yea! We wept when we remembered Zion. . . ."[15] Douglass's speech itself, with its opening praise of civil religion, recognition of suffering, and then hopeful conclusion, follows the pattern of lament given to Jews and Christians in the Psalms and the Old Testament book of Lamentations.

One observes in the book of Lamentations a variety of narrative voices offering witness to suffering. These voices include the narrator, "Daughter Zion" (the personification of Jerusalem), the strong man, the poet, and the combined voices of Jerusalem's people. Each of these voices plays a particular role in narrating Israel's pain. For example, while the narrator dispassionately begins his narration, he shifts toward an engaged participant once the voice of Daughter Zion is introduced. This is a key shift—one that brings the narrator into the role of advocate on behalf of the city. As Emmanuel Katongole notes:

> The focus of the poem shifts away from the weeping woman toward God, who is now depicted as her enemy and assaulter. The narrator does most of the speaking, but now he no longer speaks as a distant observer. He stands with her and speaks on her behalf, accusing God, whose beloved she once was, of betrayal and abuse, even of excessive and calculated rage.[16]

Frederick Douglass makes the same rhetorical move in his Fourth of July speech. He begins his speech as an observer of the American founding, chronicling the history of this revered moment by outlining the motives and measures of the American founders. He acknowledges their elevated status among his audience and praises their steadfast commitment to the founding principles. Even while expressing his respect for the founders, he simultaneously recognizes his limitations to speak about them. For, as an African American man in 1850s America, he cannot fully understand the reverence with which Americans hold slaveholding men. He therefore abandons the cause of dispassionate narration, believing that "the American side of any question may be safely left in American hands."[17]

Instead, Douglass takes up the cause of the slave in the "ever-living now," and this is where Douglass's audience would have marked a swift move from dispassionate narrator to invested ally. Similar to the narrator in Lamentations, Douglass identifies with the sufferer. He, of course, has every ability to do so as a man who has escaped the chains of bondage. Nevertheless, in freedom he had a choice. And in his choosing he chose to sympathize with those who were still in chains. "Standing there, identified with the American bondman, making his wrongs mine," he cries, "I do not hesitate to declare, with all my soul, that the character and conduct of this nation never looked blacker to me than this 4th of July!" He goes on further to note that he not only stands with the "crushed and bleeding slave" but with God himself.[18]

In Lamentations, the shift of the narrator to the co-sufferer with Daughter Zion elicits powerful emotions. "He no longer speaks as a distant observer but as an overwrought participant in Zion's unbearable suffering. He stands with her and speaks on her behalf."[19] In doing so, the narrator simultaneously signals to Daughter Zion that he sees, pays attention, and recognizes her suffering. This is exactly what Douglass does in his movement from dispassionate observer to engaged co-prosecutor.

Indeed, the witnessing of suffering is crucial to Douglass's speech. In one particularly moving passage of the speech, Douglass calls his audience to "Mark the sad procession" of slaves, "Hear" the "savage yells" of the slave driver, "see the old man," "hear a quick snap" as the whip cracks, and allow their ears to be "saluted with a scream."[20] The visceral and sensory nature of all of these words brings Douglass's audience into a position in which they must confront injustice—they must bear witness to it.

In his lament of the state of American history and its implications for the slave, Douglass also proposed a new social ethic that sought to re-orient his audience toward the pursuit of both truth and justice. In the overwhelming focus on the benefits of liberty, nineteenth century Americans were blinded to the denial of that very same liberty to millions of enslaved persons. Douglass addressed this by noting the limited vision of the founders: "Your fathers staked their lives, their fortunes, and their sacred honor, on the cause of their country. In their admiration of liberty, they lost sight of all other interests."[21] Those other interests that the founders ought to have had their sight on, according to Douglass, was the interest of freedom for all. In noting this, Douglass was simultaneously accusing both the founders and his audience, whose limited social ethic rooted in limited history had a pernicious effect on the present.

This is the value of lament in remembering the past, as many theologians have noted. Walter Brueggeman argues that "When the lament form is censured, justice questions cannot be asked and eventually become invisible and illegitimate."[22] Or, as Kathleen O'Connor puts it, "Truth does not exist if pain cannot speak."[23] For Douglass, one of the most painful aspects of Americans' unwillingness to address their difficult past was the complicity of the American church in this mis-remembering. In their twisted social ethic rooted in a limited understanding of the past, the church had come to accept the most pernicious of social evils—the Fugitive Slave Law. For Douglass, the acceptance of the Fugitive Slave Law by American Christians "implies that that church regards religion simply as a form of worship, an empty ceremony, and not a vital principle, requiring active benevolence, justice, love and good will towards man." In their absence of lament and solidarity with the suffering of others, the church had embraced injustice and failed in its witness of God's justice in the world.

The theological virtue of lament is one that has been lost in much of the American church, though it has always been central to the theology of the African American church. James Cone, Willie Jennings, Esau McCaulley, and Emmanuel Katongole have explored the relationship between lament, theology, and American History in their work, and theologians such as Soong-Chan Rah, Walter Brueggeman, and others are reclaiming it as an important theological idea.[24] Historians need to pay attention to this reclamation.

In his book *Prophetic Lament*, Soong-Chan Rah writes about the book of Lamentations and explores its implications for the twenty-first century American church. Specifically relating the importance of lament to the historical memory of American Christians, Rah notes,

For evangelical Christians riding the fumes of a previous generation's assumptions, a triumphalistic theology of celebration and privilege rooted in a praise-only narrative is perpetuated by the absence of lament and the underlying narrative of suffering that informs lament.[25]

The echoes of Douglass in this statement are difficult to miss.

In his exploration of lament, Rah outlines certain characteristics of the spirit of lament. They include:

1. A recognition of the reality of shame and death.
2. Understanding the sources of suffering in the present.
3. Seeking forms of spiritual expression that honor those who suffer.
4. A recognition of our own weakness and God's sovereignty at work in the midst of suffering.
5. Corporate recognition of and prayer over suffering.[26]

In explaining his second point—understanding the sources of present suffering—Rah has much to say about the importance of telling the truth about American history. "Often," he argues,

American Christians may even deny the narrative of suffering, claiming that things weren't so bad for the slaves or that at least the African Americans had the chance to convert to Christianity. The story of suffering is often swept under the rug in order not to create discomfort or bad feelings. Lament is denied because the dead body in front of us is being denied. But the funeral dirge genre of Lamentations 1 requires the telling of the full story of death—the cause of the death, the history surrounding that death and the historical effects of that death—because a dead body cannot be ignored.[27]

So how do we keep from ignoring the dead body in front of us? One example of right remembering and lament is the National Memorial for Peace and Justice, the memorial opened recently in Montgomery, Alabama to remember those who lost their lives to the violence of lynching during the dark days of Jim Crow. With its 800 hanging columns, each representing a county and those lynched there, the memorial leaves little room to ignore the suffering of those who were brutality maimed, tortured, and killed at the height of the racial violence in the late nineteenth and early twentieth centuries. As visitors to the memorial walk through the columns, they must walk underneath some of them, feeling the threat and oppression of the enormous metal shafts suspended above them. Turning the corner and proceeding down a walkway, visitors are then confronted with a powerful statement about the nature of history, memory, and lament:

For the hanged and beaten.
For the shot, drowned, and burned.

For the tortured, tormented, and terrorized.
For those abandoned by the rule of law.
We will remember.
With hope because hopelessness is the enemy of justice.
With courage because peace requires bravery.
With persistence because justice is a constant struggle.
With faith because we shall overcome.

Bryan Stevenson, the well-known lawyer and founder of the National Memorial for Peace and Justice, noted in an interview with the New York Times that the purpose of the Memorial was not to shame or punish, but to liberate. "I'm not interested in talking about America's history because I want to punish America," he noted, "I want to liberate America."[28] James Baldwin tied the liberation of African Americans to that of white Americans enchained by a false memory. He noted: "if the word *integration* means anything, this is what it means: that we, with love, shall force our brothers to see themselves as they are, to cease fleeing from reality and begin to change it."[29] Stevenson, Baldwin, and Douglass all understood that the work of lament had to be accompanied by hope that things could change once right remembering began to take place. For Douglass, his hope was both in institutions and ideas, especially the ideas outlined in the American Constitution. His hope was also rooted in a sense of God's love and justice revealed in Scripture. It was a hope that did not see all things, but believed all things were possible. As Douglass noted, " . . . I do not despair of this country. There are forces in operation, which must inevitably work the downfall of slavery." He expressed this hope by ending his talk with a hymn declaring God's victory of tyrants. Emmanuel Katongole and Chris Rice present a hope similar to Douglass's in their book *Reconciling all Things*. As they argue, hope and lament must be brought together for true reconciliation to occur. "Reconciliation without lament cheapens hope," they argue. "We must refuse the consolations of cheap hope."[30]

Frederick Douglass knew that a hope for a Fourth of July celebration that could include all Americans—Black and white—would come at a deep cost. That cost was the abandonment by white Americans of their hagiographic view of the American founders and the founding era. But Douglass believe that by engaging in lament, a lament rooted in the theology of Christianity, Americans could reconcile and move toward a more hopeful future. Historians of all ideological persuasions would do well to reclaim the power of lament for repentance and transformation in the spirit of Douglass. In this way, history can play a very real role in healing the wounds of the American past.

BIBLIOGRAPHY

Baldwin, James. *The Fire Next Time*. New York: Dial Press, 1963.
Becker, Carl. "Everyman His Own Historian." *American Historical Review* 37, no. 2 (January 1932): 221–36.
Blight, David. "Historians and 'Memory.'" *Common-place* 2, no. 3 (April 2002). http://www.common-place-archives.org/vol-02/no-03/author/.
Blight, David, ed. *Narrative of the Life of Frederick Douglass, an American Slave, Written by Himself, with Related Documents*. Bedford Series in History and Culture. Boston: Bedford/St. Martin's, 2017.
Brueggeman, Walter. "The Costly Loss of Lament." *Journal for the Study of the Old Testament* 36 (1986): 57–71.
Coates, Ta-Nehisi. *Between the World and Me*. New York: Spiegel & Grau, 2015.
Cone, James. *The Cross and the Lynching Tree*, Orbis reprint ed. Maryknoll, NY: 2011.
Hughes, Richard T. *Myths America Lives by: White Supremacy and the Stories That Give Us Meaning*, 2nd ed. Urbana: University of Illinois Press, 2018.
Jennings, William James. *The Christian Imagination: Theology and the Origins of Race*. New Haven: Yale University Press, 2010.
Katongole, Emmanuel. *Born From Lament: The Theology and Politics of Hope in Africa*. Grand Rapids: Eerdmans, 2017.
Katongole, Emmanuel and Chris Rice. *Reconciling all Things: A Christian Vision for Justice, Peace, and Healing*. Downers Grove, IL: IVP Books, 2008.
McCaulley, Esau. *Reading While Black: African American Biblical Interpretation as an Exercise in Hope*. Downers Grove, IL: IVP Academic, 2020.
O'Connor, Kathleen. *Lamentations and the Tears of the World*. Maryknoll, NY: Orbis Books, 2002.
Rah, Soong-Chan. *Prophetic Lament: A Call for Justice in Troubled Times*. Downers Grove, IL: IVP Books, 2015.
Robertson, Campbell. "A Lynching Memorial is Opening. The Country has Never Seen Anything Like It." *New York Times*, April 25, 2018.

NOTES

1. James Baldwin, *The Fire Next Time* (New York: Dial Press, 1963), 21.
2. Baldwin, *The Fire Next Time*, 22.
3. Frederick Douglass, "What to the Slave is the Fourth of July?," in *Narrative of the Life of Frederick Douglass, an American Slave, Written by Himself, with Related Documents*, ed. David Blight, Bedford Series in History and Culture (Boston: Bedford/St. Martin's, 2017), 148.
4. Douglass, "What to the Slave," 152.
5. Douglass, "What to the Slave," 153.
6. Richard T. Hughes, *Myths America Lives by: White Supremacy and the Stories That Give Us Meaning*, 2nd ed. (Urbana: University of Illinois Press, 2018), 10.

7. Carl Becker, "Everyman His Own Historian," *American Historical Review* 37, no. 2 (January 1932): 221–36.

8. David Blight, "Historians and 'Memory,'" *Common-place* 2, no. 3 (April 2002), http://www.common-place-archives.org/vol-02/no-03/author/.

9. Blight, "Historians and 'Memory,'" 154.

10. Blight, "Historians and 'Memory,'" 157–58.

11. Douglass, "What to the Slave," 163.

12. Douglass, "What to the Slave," 162.

13. Douglass, "What to the Slave," 155.

14. Ta-Nehisi Coates, *Between the World and Me* (New York: Spiegel & Grau, 2015), 10.

15. Douglass, "What to the Slave," 155.

16. Emmanuel Katongole, *Born From Lament: The Theology and Politics of Hope in Africa* (Grand Rapids: Eerdmans, 2017), 45.

17. Douglass, "What to the Slave," 153.

18. Douglass, "What to the Slave," 155.

19. Katongole, *Born From Lament*, 51.

20. Douglass, "What to the Slave," 158.

21. Douglass, "What to the Slave," 152.

22. Walter Brueggeman, "The Costly Loss of Lament," *Journal for the Study of the Old Testament* 36 (1986): 63–64.

23. Kathleen O'Connor, *Lamentations and the Tears of the World* (Maryknoll, NY: Orbis Books, 2002), 125.

24. See James Cone, *The Cross and the Lynching Tree,* Orbis reprint ed. (Maryknoll, NY: 2011); William James Jennings, *The Christian Imagination: Theology and the Origins of Race* (New Haven: Yale University Press, 2010); Esau McCaulley, *Reading While Black: African American Biblical Interpretation as an Exercise in Hope* (Downers Grove, IL: IVP Academic, 2020); Katongole, *Born From Lament*; Soong-Chan Rah, *Prophetic Lament: A Call for Justice in Troubled Times* (Downers Grove, IL: IVP Books, 2015).

25. Rah, *Prophetic Lament*, 24.

26. Rah, *Prophetic Lament*, 25.

27. Rah, *Prophetic Lament*, 48.

28. Campbell Robertson, "A Lynching Memorial is Opening. The Country has Never Seen Anything Like It," *New York Times*, April 25, 2018.

29. Baldwin, *The Fire Next Time*, 24.

30. Emmanuel Katongole and Chris Rice, *Reconciling all Things: A Christian Vision for Justice, Peace, and Healing* (Downers Grove, IL: IVP Books, 2008), 95.

Chapter Three

The Planet and the Pageant

John Mitchell Jr.'s Lament and W. B. Cridlin's Celebration in Richmond, Virginia, May 1922

Peter Slade

This chapter tells two stories that converge a century ago in the month of May 1922, in the city of Richmond, Virginia. The first is the story of John Mitchell Jr., the African American editor of the newspaper the *Richmond Planet*. It is a story of lament as public protest: the lamentations of an African American Christian for his community in the Nadir—the depths of Jim Crow segregation and terror—and his balancing (and unbalancing) act to keep his public voice and prosperity as Virginia's whites stripped away his political rights and protections.[1] In the pages of the *Planet,* Mitchell lamented many of the crimes and indignities white supremacy imposed upon his people. It is a story of public protest with the hope that lamenting the crimes of the present—particularly the crime of lynching—might change the future.

The second is the story of William Broaddus Cridlin, the white amateur historian who conceived of and planned the Virginia Historical Pageant. It is a story of celebration: a great public presentation of white Christian Virginian history at the zenith of the imposition of white supremacy—the passing of Virginia's racial integrity laws in 1924. It is the story of the very careful creation of public history through newspapers, parades, and plays that held no place for African Americans. Cridlin and the white civic organizers of the Pageant expended enormous energy and resources in the belief that their selective celebration of the past would inspire the post-war generation to secure a white Virginian future for the state and the nation.

Mitchell's *Planet*

On Friday evening, May 26, 1922, the fifty-eight-year-old entrepreneur and editor John Mitchell Jr. had a copy of his newspaper the *Planet* delivered to the Executive Mansion on Capitol Square in downtown Richmond just as he had every week for the past twenty-eight years.[2] It is unlikely that the succession of governors paid the broadsheet much notice. Mitchell knew this; however, delivering the paper to the mansion was Mitchell's protest: the governor of Virginia should pay attention to the voices of the African Americans who made up a third of the population of his state.[3] Above all, the governor should hear their lamentations. As Mitchell said, the editorial mission of his paper was to be "[the] mouthpiece for the groans and woes of a suffering people."[4]

Mitchell, a slight man with a certain sartorial flair, was a colorful character with no lack of self-esteem. "It's a grand thing to be on the side of the oppressed," he proclaimed; "it gives you something for which to fight."[5] As an editor on the side of the oppressed, Mitchell encouraged his people to embrace self-help and economic development while at the same time deploying public lament. As he explained to his readers thirty years earlier, "If we are downtrodden and oppressed, let us work, accumulate enough money as we can and buy land. In the meantime, let others be assigned to howl, yes howl loudly, until the American people hear our cries."[6]

Mitchell's lament was that of a Black man who had experienced the journey from the liberation of emancipation through the possibilities of Reconstruction to the imposition of a pathological segregationist system of white supremacy. Born in Richmond on July 11, 1863, the enslaved "property" of a prominent lawyer and politician, his mother Rebecca took advantage of the educational opportunities available during the period of Reconstruction and sent her son to the Richmond Normal and High School. Founded in 1867 by the Freedmen's Bureau to train Black teachers, the school gave Mitchell a rigorous classical education. He graduated top of his class in 1881.[7]

Mitchell's biographer, Ann Field Alexander, credits the Black church as the most important influence on the young Mitchell.[8] As a boy, he attended First African Baptist Church on Broad Street and was baptized in 1878 when he was fourteen.[9] Mitchell took his faith and church membership seriously. He understood both the importance of the institution of the Black church for the African American community and the standing and respectability in the community that the institution afforded him. He taught Sunday School at First Church for years and later in life became a trustee of Virginia Seminary, a Black-operated Baptist school in Lynchburg.[10]

Mitchell had no opportunity to go to college; instead, for three years he taught the Black boys and girls of Richmond in its segregated school system. In 1884, the Virginia Assembly passed the Anderson-McCormick education bill that had the effect of removing all Black male teachers from Richmond public schools. Mitchell lost his job and financial security.[11]

In December 1884, Mitchell became the owner and editor of the struggling year-old newspaper the *Planet*.[12] The enterprise was neither promising nor unique: with only 1,200 subscribers, the *Planet* was just another one of the fifty black-owned newspapers started in Virginia between 1865 and 1905.[13] What the *Planet* had going for it was a young energetic fearless editor with grand ideas. No longer employed by the State of Virginia as a teacher, Mitchell could air his opinions without constraint.

Mitchell displayed a reckless disregard for his own safety in pursuit of justice and a good story. A biographical sketch of Mitchell published in 1887 had the subheading "The gamest Negro editor on the continent—A man of grit and iron nerve."[14] The author explained, "He is a man who would walk into the jaws of death to serve his race; and his courage is a thing to be admired."[15] An incident early in Mitchell's career caught the public's imagination. In May 1886, a mob in Charlotte County took Richard Walker from the jail where he was awaiting trial for the attempted rape of a white woman and killed him. Mitchell published extensive accounts of the lynching and, for his efforts, received a letter threatening to "hang you higher than he was hung" should Mitchell "poke that infernal head of yours in this county." The twenty-two-year-old Mitchell published the threats and then took the train down to Charlotte County wearing a fine suit and a pair of Smith & Wesson revolvers. "The cowardly letter writer was nowhere in evidence," the swashbuckling Mitchell informed the readers of the *Planet*.[16] This was an audacious challenge to extralegal killing and his readers loved it. By 1896 Mitchell had built the weekly circulation to 6,400 and the *Planet* was making money.[17]

Mitchell protested lynching and injustice in the courts for the forty-five years he was the editor of the *Planet*.[18] This took extraordinary skill to balance his protest against white Virginia society's racial conventions and prejudices. A miscalculation might have resulted in the loss of the press and possibly deadly violence. Mitchell carefully picked the cases he championed to be clear instances of injustice and he never questioned the virtue of white women.[19] He also went to great lengths in his protests to flatter and appeal to both the power and moral virtue of white elites. When Governor Fitzhue Lee commuted the death sentence of a fifteen-year-old boy, Mitchell declared it "a grand act on the part of a grander man."[20]

Mitchell used his newspaper to promote his own political career. He served on Richmond's city council for eight years from 1888–1896. This gave him a ring-side seat as the white majority worked to limit Black political power in Virginia. First came the Walton Act in 1894, which handicapped illiterate voters at the polls and opened the door to massive fraud and dismissal of ballots as improperly marked. Then in 1902, the State Assembly passed a law purging the voter rolls and instituting new voter registration with a raft of new rules including a literacy test and prohibitive poll tax reducing the Black electorate in Richmond from 6,407 to just 760.[21]

As the strictures of Jim Crow tightened, Michell shifted his center of gravity away from politics and balanced his energies around building Black-owned businesses. In doing so he appeared to tamp down his radicalism and embrace much of the self-help strategy of Booker T. Washington. Indeed, Washington declared in 1907, "Mr. Mitchell is a good type of the sane and sensible businessman of our race who are doing much to win for us as a race the respect of our white neighbors."[22] As a biographer wrote of Mitchell in 1921, "It would weary the reader to tell of all his business activities. He seems to have a genius for going to the head of things with which he is identified."[23] Most notably, in January 1902, the Mechanics' Savings Bank of Richmond opened with Mitchell as one of the sixteen founders and its elected president.

Mitchell understood the success of any Black-owned business venture in Richmond, especially one as significant as a bank, required friends in the white political and economic power structure. To do so required a new balancing act. Mitchell wrote favorably of Oliver Jackson Sands, the American National Bank of Richmond president. Sands became Mitchell's "closest white confidant" and invaluable ally in the banking world.[24]

As Mitchell built his businesses, the white state legislature increased the social and economic restrictions on its Black citizens. In 1904, the General Assembly passed an "Act concerning Public Transportation" *permitting* racial segregation. The Virginia Passenger and Power Company ordered segregation on its streetcars. In April, Mitchell urged the *Planet's* readers to boycott, "Walking is good now. Stay off the street-cars."[25] The boycott mobilized the community but the many months of walking failed when in 1906 the General Assembly passed a new law *requiring* separate but equal segregation on public transport.[26]

Across the country, racist white nativism was on the rise. The genteel whites of Richmond were leery of the new populist and anti-Catholic Ku Klux Klan that sprang up in Georgia in 1915 and gained momentum from the success of D. W. Griffith's epic movie *The Birth of a Nation*. Trying to avoid too much attention, in 1921, a chapter of the Klan started in Richmond calling itself cryptically the American Civic Association.[27] Mitchell watched this growing movement with alarm. He wrote in his editorial page, "Southern white people of the right kind are increasing in numbers and those of the wrong kind are increasing in number also."[28]

After years of struggling to keep the Mechanics' Savings Bank afloat and satisfying the banking division of the State Corporation Commission with its scrutiny of Mitchell's personal finances and increasingly stringent audits, Mitchell's business balancing act was nearly at an end. On May 19, 1922, the banking division, issued an ultimatum to Mitchell and the directors: they had thirty days to present a specific plan to save the bank. Jim Crow had limited Mitchell's educational and political aspirations, finally it was stripping away his business opportunities.

With the ascendency of white supremacy, Mitchell seems to have abandoned much of his middle-aged accommodationism. He offered public support for Marcus Garvey whom he met in 1921. He invited Garvey to visit Richmond in June 1922 (the FBI opened a file on Mitchell at this time). Most surprising for a man who last held political office in 1896, Mitchell ran for governor of Virginia in 1921, challenging the white Republican candidate. He was part of a "lily-black" slate protesting the Virginia Republicans shutting out African Americans from the party and their "lily-white" ticket. Come election day, the moderate progressive—for women voting and against anyone drinking—Democratic candidate E. Lee Trinkle won handily with Mitchell not even a close third.[29]

Mitchell wasted no time courting the new governor, suggesting that if he eschewed race-baiting and stood strong against lynching, he could receive the African American vote. In May 1922, there were particularly disturbing stories of lynching in the press. "Mob in Texas Burns Three Negroes at Same Stake" screamed the headline of the *News Leader* on May 4.[30] At the same time, the NAACP was attempting to move the doomed Dyer Anti-lynching Bill through the US Congress.[31] Mitchell devoted the front page of the May 13 edition of the *Planet* to a speech made by Trinkle at Fifth Street Baptist Church. It was, according to Mitchell, "one of the most remarkable meetings of colored people ever held in the city" (though the city's white press made no mention of it). Trinkle started by telling the congregation "there never was a more considerate race, more open to encouragement than the colored people," followed by remarks against the lawlessness of lynching. The progressive governor also preached the necessity of racial segregation. "I believe that it is just as wrong for the white man to encroach on the rights of the colored people as it is for the colored man to encroach upon the rights of the white man," Trinkle told the large gathering of Black Baptists. "There is a limit for both races beyond which it is not safe for either to go."[32]

Mitchell had paid close attention to the changing dynamics of white supremacy and Black resistance. On May 26, 1922, the editorial page in the *Planet,* delivered that Friday evening to the Executive Mansion, contained Mitchell's essay on the contours of national political leadership and the decisive changes he saw underway. "Certain it is, the cringing compromising Negro leader has had his day," Mitchell concluded. "Those now upon the field of action are determined to stand and walk upright."[33]

Surrounding his article, as befitted an editorial convention of the day, was a collection of short sentences: a mixture of aphorisms, bon mots, thrifty advice, religious maxims, personal grudges, and veiled (and not so veiled) comments on the events of the week.[34] Scattered among the cant and patronizing counsel was the full-throated howl of lament and protest that had won for Mitchell the moniker "the fighting editor." Grounded in the gospel of the Black Church, he was at his fiercest when confronting the crime of murder by lynch mob:

> You cannot permit the burning of human beings alive and then profess belief in the teachings and practices of our Lord and Savior, Jesus Christ.

He advocated for African Americans, in the face of the lawless horror of the white mob, to embrace self-defense and sell their lives dearly:

> Burning human beings has become a past-time in both Texas and Georgia. If the victims had sense enough to die fighting, the cremation of their bodies while they lived would not have taken place.

He espoused a conservative Black elitism that sought to dodge white racist condemnation of all African Americans by shifting the critique away from his class:

> White people of the right kind are all right and colored folks of the right raising are all right too, but God help the other kind of both races.

However, he knew that salvation would not come from the "white people of the right kind." As he explained:

> Some white folks are all right but they have not the moral stamina to face the white folks who are all wrong.

Theologically speaking, Mitchell addressed his lamentations to God who alone would ultimately right the wrongs:

> Colored people are praying for the triumph of right. The Good Lord will answer those prayers in His own time. Wait on the Lord.

But waiting on the Lord in prayer was no passive activity for Mitchell:

> There is only one way to secure rights denied and that is to contend for them without ceasing until they are secured.

That particular evening at the end of May, Governor Elbert Lee Trinkle was entertaining the governor of West Virginia and mayors of Baltimore and Wilmington who were in town for the Virginia Pageant.[35] Surely Trinkle was too busy wrapping up the week of celebrations in the city to have had time to read Mitchell's editorial lament.

Cridlin's Pageant

The Virginia Pageant took place over six days starting on Monday, May 22, 1922. It was a massive celebration that mobilized white Richmond and cities across the state. Each day had a theme: Richmond Day, Colonial Day, Confederate Day, Spanish and World War Day, and ending with Greater Virginia Day. Long processions with horse-drawn floats and bands paraded through the streets during the day, and each night, 3,000 people attended elaborate historic themed balls at the "mammoth Coliseum at Lombardy and Broad Streets" with guests in appropriate period costumes dancing to the melodies of the Pennsylvanian Serenaders, a twelve-piece band with "a reputation for its rhythmic terpsichorean strains."[36] There was an Old Virginia Tournament held at the fairgrounds "participated in by costumed Knights, representing every section of the State";[37] and a River Regatta featuring "war canoe races" on the James.[38]

The centerpiece of the week was the Pageant Drama performed each night in a purpose-built 21,500-seat open-air amphitheater in Bryan Park with "2,000 seats in the left bleachers . . . reserved for colored people."[39] The stage itself covered two acres of hillside behind an artificial lake. More than thirty lights focused "650,000 candle power on the players." Two hundred stagehands moved the massive scenery, including a nearly full-sized sailing ship, for the arrival of the colonists in Jamestown. The stage and seating cost the Virginia Historical Pageant Association $150,000 (the equivalent of over $2.5 million today).[40]

The three-hour *Pageant of Virginia* was a huge production telling Virginia's story from the court of Queen Elizabeth in England to the surrender of Lee at Appomattox. The Pageant Association recruited the renowned Thomas Wood Stevens, the head of the drama department at Carnegie Institute of Technology, to write and direct the Pageant Drama (Stevens had written and produced the massive *Pageant and Masque of St. Louis* in 1914 that drew audiences of 100,000).[41] The cast and chorus numbered "more than 3,000 citizens of Richmond and the Old Dominion" and included soldiers from the Richmond Light Infantry Blues who added military authenticity to the battle of Chancellorsville and the surrender of Yorktown.[42] John Powell, Richmond's own internationally celebrated composer, wrote the overture.[43] The 60-piece US Navy Band from Washington DC, in a pavilion to the left of the stage, provided the music and accompanied the 1,500-voice chorus recruited from local church choirs and choral societies.[44]

Richmond's pageant was the brainchild of insurance salesman and amateur historian William Broaddus Cridlin.[45] He had originally proposed the city stage a "Week of Progress" pageant in 1916 but had shelved his idea with the onset of the First World War. In 1920, the time seemed right and a number of key civic organizations, including the Virginia Historical Society, signed on.[46] The newly-constituted Pageant Association chose the banker Oliver J. Sands as president because he was a "vigorous aggressive type" who could help raise the money for the enterprise (the same qualities that made him a useful ally to John Mitchell). Sands then invited Cridlin to serve as the Association's secretary. With leave from his employers, Cridlin accepted the full-time position of secretary of the Pageant Association on April 31, 1921, and threw himself into the herculean year-long task of organizing and promoting the pageant.[47] Described in the press as "Father of the Pageant," the heavy-set white-haired fifty-one-year-old Cridlin had a profound role in organizing and shaping its content.[48] Thomas Wood Stevens, the writer of the Pageant Drama, credited Cridlin "for [his] invaluable advice and suggestion, and for the generous manner in which Mr. Cridlin has placed at [my] disposal the historic data he had collected."[49]

William Broaddus Cridlin was born in Chesterfield County, Virginia in 1871. The oldest of five children, he grew up steeped in a world shaped by his father Ransdell White Cridlin, a Baptist preacher, educator, and Civil War veteran who had served with distinction as a chaplain in the 38th Virginia Regiment.[50] From his mother, Emma Snelling, he inherited his love of church music and a fascination with the colonial history of Virginia. It was through his mother's line that William was proud to trace his ancestry back to Walter Chiles, a Bristol trader, who arrived in Jamestown with his family sometime before 1638. William also claimed his mother's lineage went back to John Rolf and Pocahontas.[51] A talented pianist, Cridlin had degrees in music from Richmond College and the University of Pennsylvania.[52] The income of a music teacher and church organist did not support his wife and their seven children. To make ends meet he discovered he had an aptitude for sales—first pianos and then insurance.[53]

W.B. Cridlin fancied himself a man of letters and a historian.[54] It is in this capacity as an ardent amateur that he most clearly embraced and energetically promoted many of the central interests of his caste, class, and generation. A member of the Virginia Historical Society, he devoted himself to tracing the lineage of the state's oldest white families.[55] Cridlin's genealogical work came in part from a fascination he shared with the white elites of Virginia in tracing their ancestry back to real or imagined illustrious English forebears.[56] This obsession was clearly on display in the preparation for the Pageant. The call for nominations went out a full year ahead of time for the Queen of the Pageant. "Any white girl of Virginia is eligible," she just had to send in her photograph, name, and address.[57] Of course, the woman chosen could not be just "any white girl." The winner, Mrs. Harry J. Semones, "was Miss Anderson before her marriage, her people being prominent in Southwest Virginia." Cridlin had to explain that her foreign-sounding married name came from "French-Huguenots who came to Virginia several hundred years ago."[58] By the month of the Pageant, Mrs. Semones's lineage had obviously improved. "Queen of Pageant Traces Her Ancestry Back to Edward I" crowed the headline in the *Times-Dispatch*.[59]

Cridlin had loftier ambitions for his pageant than simply affirming the historic origins of white Virginia society. When he proposed the Week of Progress in 1916, he was hoping his city would join one of the most popular artistic movements of the Progressive Era. Historian David Glassberg explains, "essential to the progressive appeal [of pageants] was the use of historical imagery to discover or invent an appropriate tradition in support of reform."[60]

What progressive reforms did Cridlin, Sands, and the Pageant Association hope to achieve through the week of celebration? Their first goal was common to all pageants: to promote civic pride and engagement and to generate income for the city. The Association promoted the Pageant as "Virginia's first great 'Home Coming Week' and the editor of the *Times-Dispatch* expressed the wish that "all those who have left the State to seek fortune elsewhere" would come back for the Pageant and decide to return for good.[61]

Another hope of the Pageant Association was more specific to the region: to promote a new self-understanding of Virginia to the state and the nation. Cridlin believed that his presentation of the story of Virginia offered an alternative and superior account of the birth of the country than the one familiar to America's school children: "These forbears came-not as exiles fleeing from religious persecution, but volunteers, dreaming of self-government; of liberty."[62] The architects of the Pageant clearly wished to establish that the secession of Virginia from the Union and joining the Confederacy should be understood in continuity with—not a tragic break from—Virginians' greatness, their love of freedom, and their singular importance in establishing and maintaining the Republic. In the iconography of the Pageant, General Robert E. Lee's portrait took equal place alongside other great Virginians: John Smith, George Washington, and Woodrow Wilson. This meant that the "Lost Cause" was not lost at all, it just needed to be placed in the context of the long triumphant history of Virginia: The Confederacy was just one of the causes championed by white Virginians in the relentless progress of a free and liberty-loving people.

Finally, the Pageant was intended to inspire current and future generations of white Virginians to emulate their forebears and form their state, country, and world in their image. The Pageant Drama closed with The Spirit of Virginia (a white woman draped in a toga) addressing her citizens:

> This high charge I give unto my children:
>
> Forget not; fail not; shape the years to come
>
> That those who gave us our great heritage
>
> Shall not be shamed.[63]

With the Pageant Week reaching its end, John Mitchell Jr. offered his judgment on the great celebration. In contrast to the pages of coverage in the white papers, Mitchell wrote only two short paragraphs that week in the editorial page of the *Planet*. Perhaps this was a judicious silence as Oliver J. Sands was the president of the Pageant Association and Mitchell, if he had any hope of reversing his business fortunes, needed his powerful white friend to vouch for his financial acumen with the banking division. "The Virginia Historical Pageant has passed into history as one of the best staged affairs ever seen here," praised Mitchell. However, the newspaperman in him could not let injustice against his people go unremarked. Mitchell quietly inserted his lament amid hyperbolic praise and promise of African American support. "As a citizen of Richmond, interested in its welfare and anxious about its prosperity, we [African Americans] realize that the success of the venture was our success, even though we had *no active participation* in this superb achievement of the progressive white citizens of this locality."[64] The Association had not invited any Black civic organizations to participate in the processions but Mitchell's three-word critique cut much deeper. It pointed to a startling omission in the Pageant Drama: in the dramatic presentation of the story of Virginia, African Americans were entirely absent.[65] Incredibly, there was no mention or portrayal of slavery and no suggestion that African Americans had any role, active or passive, in the state's history.

W.B. Cridlin and the Pageant audience were of course very aware of the presence of African Americans in Virginia and at least some of the role they played in its history. Cridlin was personally acquainted through his family with their suffering. The 1840 census shows that both of Cridlin's parents grew up in households that included enslaved people. And, in 1885 while a student in Richmond, his father R.W. Cridlin preached at the funeral of a murdered white girl. Moved from grief to vengeance by his words, the congregation became a lynch mob.[66]

Cridlin's excising of African Americans from the history of Virginia is also evident in his *A History of Colonial Virginia* published by the Pageant

Association. African Americans receive explicit mention in only two of its 140 pages of historical narrative.[67]

The exclusion of African Americans from both the production and content of the Pageant is thrown into stark relief by the significant inclusion of Native Americans. W.B. Cridlin believed himself to have great sympathy for Virginia's original inhabitants. He wrote that he had "the desire to do justice to a race that has received little sympathy at the hands of many of our historians."[68] He wanted to present "the history of their race, its trials and tragedies, without the prejudice of the past centuries, with that Christian charity they so oft times richly deserve."[69] In preparation for the Pageant, the papers reported that "[the] heads of several tribes of Red Men in Richmond held a pow-wow with Secretary W.B. Cridlin."[70] His efforts resulted in "A group of Chickohiminy [sic] Indians headed by Chief O.W. Adkins" marching in the Colonial Parade. The *News-Leader* reported that "there were about twenty in the party, all dressed in their native regalia and dabbed with war paint in real redskin style."[71] It is unlikely that the watching crowds shared Cridlin's well-intentioned but problematic "Christian charity"; they likely just saw the curious remnants of a long-vanquished "savage" foe.

Native Americans also had a major role in the Pageant Drama, though white Virginians played them in red face. Stevens and Cridlin prided themselves on the play's historical authenticity. Bizarrely, in the scene where Pocahontas meets the captive John Smith, "Miss Katherine Pleasants, a member of the Colonial Dames and a popular member of Richmond society," had to deliver most of her lines in "the vocabulary of Indian words given by Captain Smith in his 'Voyages and Discoveries.'"[72]

Cridlin, like many white Virginians, had a fascination with Pocahontas who featured prominently in the Drama and on several of the floats in the parades. She had a central and complex role in their mythology of race, conquest, and destiny as a savior figure who legitimized and ennobled the colonists' claim on the land.[73] "See here the little maid who saved the town," proclaimed the Pageant's narrator, "wooed, won and wed to make a living link between the red folk and her Englishmen."[74] W.B. Cridlin explained why the connection with Pocahontas and John Rolfe was so desirable in the society of his day: "their descendants have ever occupied an eminent position in the Old Dominion. Many prominent families are proud of direct descent from this Indian princess."[75]

Reading contemporaneous accounts of the Pageant you can see an overlap emerging between the old white obsession with ancestry and the new scientific racism based on the developing science of genetics. One white citizen of Richmond wrote at the end of the Pageant that he hoped all the school children learned, "the slow but certain growth of the principles of civilization as outlined by the hardy settlers, who filled with the best blood of the Anglo-Saxon, came to plant their banners of freedom." And "the same blood that infused the veins of John Smith and all the others of that period . . . still flows through the veins of real Virginians."[76] Blood enhanced for the chosen few, one could add, with a real or imagined microdose of Pocahontas's DNA.

Deeply concerned to preserve the purity of this "best blood" from contamination, just five months after the Pageant, a small but determined group of white Virginians broke from the Ku Klux Klan and formed the Anglo-Saxon Clubs.[77] Spearheaded by none other than John Powell, the composer of the Pageant's overture, the Anglo-Saxon Clubs were a highly successful lobbying organization raising the alarm that miscegenation would bring about the collapse of Anglo-Saxon civilization.[78]

We do not know whether Cridlin himself embraced the scientific racism of the Anglo-Saxon Clubs or supported the campaign to criminalize marriage between races but it is impossible to imagine this campaign would have succeeded had white Virginians not embraced the story he presented in the Pageant.[79] Those who absorbed the fable that their "race" had a unique providential destiny to advance democracy and even civilization itself easily took the next step: clearly it is important to preserve the unique features of that race—cultural and genetic—against those who would adulterate it. Many agreed with the *Times-Dispatch* editorial in July 1923 that proclaimed: "We of the white race have been disposed to shut our eyes to the menace of Negro amalgamation . . . In the South we have fought for supremacy, that being the pressing urgent issue forgetting the while the more insidious less apparent problem of integrity."[80]

On March 24, 1924, Governor E. Lee Trinkle signed the Racial Integrity Act into state law. In its wording, you can see the harsh eugenic logic and scientific racism of the Anglo-Saxon Clubs meeting the romantic mythology presented in the Pageant. The Racial Integrity Act decreed that it was "unlawful for any white person in this State to marry any save a white person" and crucially redefined "white" as "such person as has no trace whatever of any blood other than Caucasian." But for all those genealogically obsessed aristocratic Virginians, it included a concession that became known as the Pocahontas clause: "Persons who have one-sixteenth or less of the blood of the American Indian and have no other non-caucasic blood shall be deemed white persons."[81]

Lament and Celebration

This chapter only introduces these stories of African American lament and white celebration. Readers can draw their own conclusions about the bravery, bravado, and accommodation behind John Mitchell's lament as well as the motivations, impact, and historical selectivity of W. B. Cridlin's pageant. If the stories hold any meaning for the reader, it will be far more expansive and untidy than will fit neatly in a historian's thesis.[82] It is not hard, for example, to find resonances between these century-old stories and the contemporary and concurrent tales of lament over the death of Black lives that mattered and insistent attempts to preserve and celebrate a version of American history exclusively centered around 1776. I will, however, offer this: The Pageant was an attempt to impose an exclusively white myth of Virginia's past onto the state's future. Black triumphs, victories, joys, defeats, and suffering literally had no part in this history or this future. The celebration in Richmond in 1922 was part of a process of creating and maintaining a racialized structure of white historical memory that was acoustically dead to the intrusive sounds of African American lament. To people living inside this mythologized memory—the house that Cridlin, and so many others, built and celebrated—African American voices raised in lament, if they were heard at all, sounded as though they came from outside.

Postscript

Following the Pageant, W.B. Cridlin continued in his role as public historian and genealogist of white Virginia. In 1923, he accepted the position of Registrar of the Virginia Society of Sons of the American Revolution and that same year, the Sons of Confederate Veterans commissioned him their "Assistant Historian-in-Chief."[83] In 1924 he became the Virginia campaign director for the Thomas Jefferson Memorial Foundation raising money from school children one penny at a time to purchase Monticello for the nation.[84] He died of a heart attack on July 5, 1932 at his home in the suburbs of Richmond. He was sixty-one years old. The death certificate recorded his trade as "Refrigerator Salesman." An obituary in the *Farmville Herald* noted: "He was director of the Virginia Historical Pageant and it was during that work that he suffered a breakdown, from which he never recovered."[85]

On July 15, 1922, the banking division shut the Black-owned Mechanic's Savings Bank for business. In August, the police arrested Mitchell on eighteen counts of fraud and theft including "embezzlement, falsification of records, and theft of bank funds."[86] On April 30, 1923, the court sentenced him to three years in jail. Mitchell made bail and the fighting editor and his lawyers managed to get the Supreme Court of Appeals to drop all charges in March 1925. Mitchell was, however, never able to rescue his bank from receivership but he did continue as owner and editor of the *Planet* until his death at sixty-six on December 3, 1929. His last words were, "I am ready for you death."[87]

BIBLIOGRAPHY

Acts of the General Assembly of the State of Virginia, Commencing January 9, 1924, An Act to preserve racial integrity, S.B. 219, approved March 20, 1924.

Alexander, Ann Field. *Race Man: The Rise and Fall of the "Fighting Editor," John Mitchell Jr.* Charlottesville, VA: University of Virginia Press, 2002.

Caldwell, Arthur Bunyan, ed. *History of the American Negro and His Institutions, Virginia Edition.* Atlanta: A.B. Caldwell Publishing Company, 1921.

Cridlin, William Broaddus. *A History of Colonial Virginia: The First Permanent Colony in America.* Richmond, VA: Williams Printing Co., 1923.

Cridlin, William Broaddus. *Thomas Jefferson, Patriot, Statesman, Scientist.* Thomas Jefferson Memorial Foundation, Inc, 1924.

Cridlin, William Broaddus. "Virginia Historical Pageant." *The Virginia Magazine of History and Biography* 30, no. 2 (April 1922): 119-22.

Doktor, Stephanie Delane. "How a White Supremacist Became Famous for His Black Music: John Powell and Rhapsodie Negre (1918)." *American Music* 38 (2020): 395-427.

Glassberg, David. *American Historical Pageantry: The Uses of Tradition in the Early Twentieth Century.* Chapel Hill, NC: UNC Press, 1990.

González, Juan and Joseph Torres. *News for All the People: The Epic Story of Race and the American Media.* Verso Books, 2011.

Jones, J. William. *Christ in the Camp: Or, Religion in Lee's Army.* Richmond, VA: B. F. Johnson & Co., 1887.

"Officers and Members of the Virginia Historical Society." *The Virginia Magazine of History and Biography* 28, no. 1 (January 1920): i-xiii.

"Personals." *Richmond College Messenger* 19, no. 2 (November 1892); 32.

"Princess Anne County Confederate Statue Roundtable Meeting Notes–May 4, 2018." April 26, 2019, 11. https://www.vbgov.com/government/departments/planning/boards-commissions-committees/Documents/VA%20Historical%20Preservation/Confederate%20Statue/05042018%20PACCSR%20Meeting%20Notes%20Approved%20as%20Corrected.pdf.

Sherman, Richard B. "'The Last Stand': The Fight for Racial Integrity in Virginia in the 1920s." *The Journal of Southern History* 54, no. 1 (1988), 69–92.

Simmons, C. A. *The African American Press: A History of News Coverage during National Crises, with Special Reference to Four Black Newspapers, 1827–1965.* Jefferson, NC: McFarland & Company, Inc., 1998.

Simmons, William J. *Men of Mark: Eminent, Progressive and Rising.* Cleveland, OH: G. M. Rewell & Company, 1887.

Smith, Douglas. "The Campaign for Racial Purity and the Erosion of Paternalism in Virginia, 1922–1930: 'Nominally White, Biologically Mixed, and Legally Negro.'" *The Journal of Southern History* 68, no. 1 (2002): 65-106.

Stevens, Thomas Wood. *Book of Words: The Pageant of Virginia.* Virginia Historical Pageant Association, 1922.

Suggs, Henry Lewis, ed. *The Black Press in the South, 1865–1979.* Westport, CT: Greenwood Press, 1983.

Taylor, George B. *Virginia Baptist Ministers*. Lynchburg, VA: J. Bell Company Inc., 1915.
Thomas Wood Stevens Papers, 1895–1984. Arizona Archives Online. http://www.azarchivesonline.org/xtf/view?docId=ead/uoa/UAMS002.xml.
U.S. Census Bureau. State Compendium Virginia, 1925. https://www2.census.gov/prod2/decennial/documents/06229686v44-49ch2.pdf.
Virginia Republican Party. "All-Black Republican Ticket of 1921." Special Collections, 1921, Ms2008–058, University Libraries, Virginia Tech. https://encyclopediavirginia.org/13656-121bbf10f9bcdaf/.Walther, Hans-Jürgen. Hamburg Philharmonia Orchestra, *John Powell - Ouverture "In Old Virginia" Op.28 (1921)*, Record, 1955. https://www.youtube.com/watch?v=t25d8RDWzmQ.
Washington, Booker T. *The Negro in Business*. Chicago: Hertel, Jenkins & Company, 1907.
White, Melvin R. "Thomas Wood Stevens: Creative Pioneer." *Educational Theatre Journal* 3, no. 4 (1951): 280-93.
Woodley, Randy S. *Indigenous Theology and the Western Worldview: A Decolonized Approach to Christian Doctrine*. Acadia Studies in Bible and Theology. Ada, OK: Baker Academic, 2022.
Woodley, Randy. *Jesus and Pocahontas: Gospel, Mission, and National Myth*. Eugene, OR: Cascade Books, 2015.

NOTES

1. The idea of Mitchell balancing competing forces comes from Ann Field Alexander, Race Man: The Rise and Fall of the "Fighting Editor," John Mitchell Jr (Charlottesville, VA: University of Virginia Press, 2002), 185.

2. Alexander, Race Man, 53.

3. U.S. Census Bureau, State Compendium Virginia, 1925, https://www2.census.gov/prod2/decennial/documents/06229686v44-49ch2.pdf.

4. John Mitchell Jr. et al. to O 'Ferrall, September 12, 1894 in Alexander, Race Man, 33.

5. *Richmond Planet*, June 13, 1891 in Alexander, *Race Man*, 47.

6. *Richmond Planet*, January 3, 1891 in Alexander, Race Man, 40.

7. William J. Simmons, *Men of Mark: Eminent, Progressive and Rising* (Cleveland, OH: G. M. Rewell & Company, 1887), 316.

8. Alexander, *Race Man*, 9.

9. Alexander, *Race Man*, 11.

10. Alexander, *Race Man*, 119.

11. Alexander, *Race Man*, 30.

12. Henry Lewis Suggs, ed., *The Black Press in the South, 1865–1979*, vol. 45 (Westport, CT: Greenwood Press, 1983), 392.

13. Suggs, *The Black Press in the South,* 379.

14. Simmons, *Men of Mark*, 314.

15. Simmons, *Men of Mark*, 320.

16. Alexander, *Race Man*, 42.

17. Suggs, *The Black Press in the South*, 393; Alexander, Race Man, 36.

18. Charles A. Simmons notes the correlation between the expansion of the Black press and the rise in lynching. Between 1895 and 1915 a total of 1,290 Black newspapers started. Between 1889 and 1918, the NAACP recorded 3,224 lynchings; 2,522 were African Americans. C. A. Simmons, *The African American Press: A History of News Coverage during National Crises, with Special Reference to Four Black Newspapers, 1827–1965* (Jefferson, NC: McFarland & Company, Inc., 1998), 21.

19. Alexander, *Race Man*, 66. This is in contrast to Ida B. Wells, the famous crusading journalist and Mitchell's contemporary, who had to flee Memphis in 1889 after suggesting in print that white women might be fabricating charges of rape to cover incidents of consensual sex with Black men. Simmons, *The African American Press*, 16–19; Juan González and Joseph Torres, News for All the People: The Epic Story of Race and the American Media (Verso Books, 2011), 169.

20. Alexander, *Race Man*, 46.

21. There was an exception if you were a veteran of the US or Confederate army or the son of a veteran. Alexander, Race Man, 114–16.

22. Booker T. Washington, *The Negro in Business* (Chicago: Hertel, Jenkins & Company, 1907), 124-25.

23. Arthur Bunyan Caldwell, ed., *History of the American Negro and His Institutions, Virginia Edition*, vol. 5 (Atlanta: A.B. Caldwell Publishing Company, 1921), 125.

24. Alexander, *Race Man*, 159; Caldwell, *History of the American Negro and His Institutions*, 124.

25. *Richmond Planet*, April 16, 1904, 3.

26. Alexander, *Race Man*, 132–41.

27. "200 Men Turned Away From John Marshall High School Building," Richmond *Times-Dispatch*, July 31, 1921, 10.

28. *Richmond Planet*, May 27, 1922, 4.

29. Alexander, *Race Man*, 186–91; Virginia Republican Party, "All-Black Republican Ticket of 1921," Special Collections, 1921, Ms2008–058, University Libraries, Virginia Tech, https://encyclopediavirginia.org/13656-121bbf10f9bcdaf/.

30. "Mob in Texas Burns Three Negroes at Same Stake," Richmond *News Leader*, May 4, 1922, 1; "Cremation of Trio Follows Girl's Murder," Richmond *News Leader*, May 6, 1922, 1; "Pastor and Sheriff Plead Vainly to Stop Lynching," Richmond *News Leader*, May 19, 1922, 1; "Negro Burned at Stake for Murder of Woman," Richmond *Times-Dispatch*, May 19, 1922, 8; "Mob Resumes Hunt for Accused Negro," Richmond *Times-Dispatch*, May 20, 1922, 1.

31. "Assert Antilynching Bill Unconstitutional," Richmond *Times-Dispatch*, May 24, 1922, 2.

32. "Gov. Trinkle Speaks to the Colored People," *Richmond Planet*, May 13, 1922, 1, 3.

33. "A Word About Leadership," *Richmond Planet*, May 27, 1922, 4.

34. *Richmond Planet*, May 27, 1922, 4.

35. "Two Governors will be in Parade Tomorrow," Richmond *Times-Dispatch*, May 25, 1922, 3.

36. "Pageant Balls to Eclipse Any Yet Seen," Richmond *Times-Dispatch*, May 21, 1922, Section 3, 5.

37. William Broaddus Cridlin, "Virginia Historical Pageant," The Virginia Magazine of History and Biography 30, no. 2 (April 1922): 121.

38. "Usher in Pageant with Grand March of Military Units," Richmond *Times-Dispatch*, May 14, 1922, 17.

39. "Pageant Prices," Richmond *News Leader*, May 20, 1922, 1.

40. "Capitol Square Barely Would Accommodate Amphitheater," Richmond *Times-Dispatch*, May 26, 1922, 3.

41. David Glassberg, *American Historical Pageantry: The Uses of Tradition in the Early Twentieth Century* (Chapel Hill, NC: UNC Press, 1990), 192, 239. Between 1909 and 1941 Stevens was the author and director of some forty or more pageants. Melvin R. White, "Thomas Wood Stevens: Creative Pioneer," Educational Theatre Journal 3, no. 4 (1951): 287. Also see Thomas Wood Stevens papers, 1895–1984, Arizona Archives Online, http://www.azarchivesonline.org/xtf/view?docId=ead/uoa/UAMS002.xml.

42. "Twenty Odd Scenes Show Big Moments," Richmond *News Leader*, May 20, 1922, 1; "Blues Play Prominent Part in Pageant Scenes," Richmond *Times-Dispatch*, May 26, 1922, 3.

43. Thomas Wood Stevens, Book of Words: The Pageant of Virginia (Virginia Historical Pageant Association, 1922), 8. In 1921, John Powell finished his eleven-minute overture "In Old Virginia" Op.28. Archived correspondence indicates he wrote the overture following a request from the Plymouth Pageant. This must have been the overture used for the Virginia Pageant. "Letter, George P. Baker to John Powell," Papers of John Powell 1921, Box-folder 4:1, Albert and Shirley Small Special Collections Library, University of Virginia, https://ead.lib.virginia.edu/vivaxtf/view?docId=uva-sc/viu03212.xml. You can listen to a recording on YouTube Hans-Jürgen Walther, Hamburg Philharmonia Orchestra, John Powell - Ouverture "In Old Virginia" Op.28 (1921), Record, 1955, https://www.youtube.com/watch?v=t25d8RDWzmQ.

44. Cridlin, "Virginia Historical Pageant," 121; Richmond *News Leader*, May 30, 1922, 17; "Pageant Pointers," Richmond *News Leader*, May 3, 1922, 1.

45. Cridlin is my wife's great-grandfather. Interestingly, there is no family lore concerning the Pageant.

46. "City Organizers Will Meet December 28 to Plan Historical Pageant," Richmond *News Leader*, December 18, 1920, 16.

47. "W.B. Cridlin Will Accept Pageant Secretaryship," Richmond *Times-Dispatch*, May 1, 1921, 1.

48. "Sands and Cridlin Share Chief Honors for Pageant," Richmond *News Leader*, May 30, 1922, 17.

49. Stevens, *Book of Words: The Pageant of Virginia*, 9.

50. George B. Taylor, *Virginia Baptist Ministers* (Lynchburg, VA: J. Bell Company Inc., 1915), 381; J. William Jones, *Christ in the Camp: Or, Religion in Lee's Army* (Richmond, VA: B. F. Johnson & Co., 1887), 480.

51. William Broaddus Cridlin, "Lineage of Pocahontas," a one page unpublished genealogy is in the possession of the author.

52. "Personals," Richmond College Messenger 19, no. 2 (November 1892): 32; "Music Teacher," *Farmville Herald*, July 1, 1898, 3.

53. "Manchester News," Richmond *News Leader*, November 1903, 8; "Has a Hundred Men in Service," Richmond *Times-Dispatch*, December 30, 1917, 9.

54. "Young Dramatist Here," Richmond *News Leader*, May 20, 1903, 8.

55. "Officers and Members of the Virginia Historical Society," *The Virginia Magazine of History and Biography* 28, no. 1 (January 1920), vi.

56. J. Douglas Smith, "The Campaign for Racial Purity and the Erosion of Paternalism in Virginia, 1922–1930: 'Nominally White, Biologically Mixed, and Legally Negro,'" The Journal of Southern History 68, no. 1 (2002): 66.

57. "Choose Queen for Pageant," Richmond *News Leader*, May 30, 1921, 1.

58. "Pageant Queen Bears French Name," *Highland Recorder*, December 9, 1921, 1.

59. "Queen of Pageant Traces Her Ancestry Back to Edward I," Richmond *Times-Dispatch*, May 21, 1922, 8.

60. Glassberg, *American Historical Pageantry*, 4.

61. "Richmond Nation's Mecca As Hosts Begin To Come For Historical Pageant," Richmond *Times-Dispatch*, May 21, 1922, 1, 2.

62. Cridlin, "Virginia Historical Pageant," 119.

63. Stevens, *Book of Words*, 144. See also Thomas Wood Stevens Papers, 1895–1984, Arizona Archives Online, http://www.azarchivesonline.org/xtf/view?docId=ead/uoa/UAMS002.xml.

64. *Richmond Planet*, May 27, 1922, 4, (emphasis added).

65. While there were no Black characters in the Pageant proper, from the script, there appear to have been two minor characters included in the stand-alone scenes performed after the Pageant on their themed night. The first was the "Old doorkeeper" at William and Mary who appeared once on Williamsburg night, and "Caesar" the "old colored servant" who helped students on University of Virginia night. Both characters were probably played by white students in black face. Stevens, *Book of Words: The Pageant of Virginia*, 94, 105.

66. "Swung from a Tree," *Richmond Dispatch*, November 17, 1885, 2; "Noah Cherry Lynched," *Norfolk Virginian*, 40, no. 151, November 17, 1885, 1, in "Princess Anne County Confederate Statue Roundtable Meeting Notes–May 4, 2018," April 26, 2019, 11, https://www.vbgov.com/government/departments/planning/boards-commissions-committees/Documents/VA%20Historical%20Preservation/Confederate%20Statue/05042018%20PACCSR%20Meeting%20Notes%20Approved%20as%20Corrected.pdf.

67. He briefly mentions "the first negroes brought to the colony arrived in 1619" and another couple of mentions of the "twenty negroes" brought as cargo to Virginia later in the chapter. William Broaddus Cridlin, *A History of Colonial Virginia: The*

First Permanent Colony in America (Richmond, VA: Williams Printing Co., 1923), 62, 81.

68. Cridlin, *A History of Colonial Virginia*, 72.

69. Cridlin, *A History of Colonial Virginia*, 23.

70. "Tribes of Red Men to Aid the Pageant," *Highland Recorder*, September 30, 1921, 1.

71. "Parade With Many Floats Is Beautiful," Richmond *News Leader*, May 23, 1922, 1, 22.

72. Photograph caption, Richmond *Times-Dispatch*, May 7, 1922, Society Section, 3; Stevens, *Book of Words*, 27.

73. For a detailed study of the power of the Pocahontas myth, see Howard A. Snyder and Randy Woodley, *Jesus and Pocahontas: Gospel, Mission, and National Myth* (Eugene, OR: Cascade Books, 2015).

74. Stevens, *Book of Words*, 41.

75. Cridlin, *A History of Colonial Virginia*, 51.

76. Kenneth McCoy Tucker, "Pageant as Seen Through Eyes of High School Student," Richmond *Times-Dispatch*, May 26, 1922.

77. "Ku-Klux Klan Here Acts to Break Up Order in Nation," Richmond *Times-Dispatch*, October 18, 1922, 1.

78. Richard B. Sherman, "'The Last Stand': The Fight for Racial Integrity in Virginia in the 1920s," *The Journal of Southern History* 54, no. 1 (1988): 77; Stephanie Delane Doktor, "How a White Supremacist Became Famous for His Black Music: John Powell and Rhapsodie Negre (1918)," *American Music* 38 (2020): 395-427.

79. There are other instances of progressive Pageantry enabling racist legislation. Glassberg connects the St Louis Pageant of 1914 and of "united public spirit that would foster the enactment of lasting municipal reforms" and its "virtual exclusion of black St. Louis" with the passage of a segregated housing ordinance in 1916. Glassberg, *American Historical Pageantry*, 195–97.

80. "Racial Integrity," Richmond *Times-Dispatch*, July 22, 1923, quoted in "Racial Integrity," *Richmond Planet*, July 28, 1923, 4. J. Douglas Smith shows how the white elites who embraced racial paternalism didn't openly support the Anglo-Saxon Clubs, seeing them as racial agitators; however,"[they] never questioned the essential rightness and necessity of racial integrity." Smith, "The Campaign for Racial Purity and the Erosion of Paternalism in Virginia, 1922–1930," 69.

81. Acts of the General Assembly of the State of Virginia, Commencing January 9, 1924, An Act to preserve racial integrity, S.B. 219, approved March 20, 1924.

82. This is an acknowledgement that the western academy harnesses (and thereby limits) stories to a thesis. "Most Western communicative practices rely on story as a filler or as a way of emphasizing propositional communications." Randy S. Woodley, *Indigenous Theology and the Western Worldview: A Decolonized Approach to Christian Doctrine*, Acadia Studies in Bible and Theology (Ada, OK: Baker Academic, 2022), xi.

83. The Sons of Confederate Veterans commissioning certificate is in the possession of the author.

84. William Broaddus Cridlin, *Thomas Jefferson, Patriot, Statesman, Scientist* (Thomas Jefferson Memorial Foundation, Inc, 1924).
85. "William B. Cridlin Dies in Richmond," *Farmville Herald*, July 8, 1932, 1.
86. Alexander, *Race Man*, 195.
87. Alexander, *Race Man*, 203.

Chapter Four

"I'm tired of funerals. I'm tired of it! We've got to stand up!"

Collective Lament, Collective Anger and Collective Action in the Civil Rights Struggle

Ansley Quiros

"Lament," as Soon-Chan Rah simply puts it, "is the language of suffering."[1] Whether screams on ancient battlefields, whispers in hospital rooms, or weeping on couches drenched with tears, lament has always been a feature of human life. Biblical lament is distinct from an abstract feeling of sorrow or sadness, rooted rather in specific conditions of loss, grief and humiliation, in "the context of tragedy."[2] It is an outpouring of wrenching pain before God and also, as Rah writes, an "act of protest." The lamenter," he continues," is allowed to express indignation and even outrage about the experience of suffering."[3] Lament is not an expression of neat theodicy, but wailing, screaming, pounding fists on pulpits. It is raw. Lament can also be both and personal and communal, even, as Kathleen O'Connor points out, "national."[4] This shared lament usually comes in response to historical injustice and serves as a collective balm and a catalyst for change within a theological frame. In the American context, we see this nowhere as clearly as within the Black Christian tradition, particularly within the long Black freedom movement.

Enslaved and subjugated, the historical experiences of Black Americans are undoubtedly full of horrific oppression. And yet, Black Christians have resisted throughout, insisting on their belovedness and cultivating, in faith, a robust theological imagination. During the civil rights era, as in generations before, Black Americans were killed by white supremacists and their hideous idolatries. These awful tragedies produced personal and collective lament that, in turn, galvanized local communities and even the nation. Analyzing the responses to the murders of Emmett Till, James Chaney, and Jimmie Lee Jackson, we can see how grief was practiced within a theological tradition of lament that propelled protest movements.

To do this we will have to go to the gravesides, to the place of the funeral dirge. "The tragedy of our racial history," Rah asserts, "requires the lament of the funeral dirge."[5] It is the place of honest lament, a space that "does not allow for the denial of death nor . . . culpability in that death."[6] The dead bodies, the fact of Emmett Till, James Chaney, and Jimmie Lee Jackson's slain corpses, cannot be denied, nor the forces that killed them.[7] So together, we will examine the historical realities that led to these murders and participate in the dirges.[8] With Mamie Till Bradley, we will look at the horrors of what white supremacy wrought on Black children, with Fannie Lee Chaney and David Dennis we will rage at inaction, and with the Jackson family, we will march. With them, we will faithfully lament before God. Perhaps it will inspire us, like these in the civil rights era, to persistent faith, or righteous anger, or holy action in our day.

Of note: Many of the lamenters are mothers. This has Biblical and historical precedence. Though scholars generally agree that the author of Lamentations is the prophet Jeremiah, a female voice narrates much of the book, Daughter Zion, the Daughter of Jerusalem.[9] The voice of lament is female since, according to Rah, "women's voices rise up to express the depth of sorrow experienced by the community."[10] As we consider Black lament, a communal experience, we will listen to specific lamenters, many of them women, give voice to that experience.

Mamie Till Bradley was at home on Chicago's South Side when she got the call. At the beginning of that summer of 1955, she had sent her fourteen-year-old son Emmett Till, who she called Bobo, to stay with extended family in Money, Mississippi, a tiny community of less than 400 in Leflore County, right in the heart of the Delta.

Moses Wright, Mamie's uncle and Emmett's great uncle, had come up to visit, and then made the offer to take Till and his cousin Wheeler Parker down South for a few weeks. Emmett had wanted to go. So Mamie Till kissed her son goodbye, gave him his late father's signet ring, and sent him off. Over the next few weeks, the kids enjoyed themselves together—telling stories, exploring, going fishing, even helping out working in the cotton fields. Till wrote to his mother in careful cursive on August 27: "Dear Mom, How is everybody? I hope you and Jean is fine. I hope you had a nice trip. I am having a fine time, will be home next week. Please have my motorbike fixed for me (pay you back). If I get any mail, put it up for me . . . everybody here is fine and having a good time . . . your son, Bobo." The next day he was gone, kidnapped and murdered.[11]

As the now-familiar account goes, Emmett Till, his cousins and some neighborhood kids had decided to stop at Bryant's Grocery Store a few days earlier. While there, Carolyn Bryant, a "black haired, brown eyed" high school beauty queen, and the 21-year-old wife of the store's owner Roy Bryant, claimed Till "wolf whistled" or made "ugly remarks" to her, or in some accounts even grabbed her. While the details are disputed, as is the possibility that Carolyn Bryant has since admitted she lied,[12] what's certain is there was a perceived violation of the strict laws and mores forbidding social and sexual contact across races in Mississippi. A few days later, Roy Bryant and his half-brother J.W. Milam took Emmett from his aunt and uncle's house in the night to exact revenge. Over their wails and pleading, they claimed that the boy would be returned if he wasn't "the right one." Two days later, Till still missing, Bryant and Milam were arrested with promises that they'd be let go when he was found. But where was Emmett Till? As Sheriff Smith put it, that was the "$64 question."[13]

Emmett Till, of course, was dead, brutally murdered.[14] A fisherman discovered his body in the Tallahatchie River on August 31, who then alerted authorities. Eventually the news reached his mother.

Mamie Till Bradley was "so shocked and so upset she didn't know what to do." She went to her mother and father's house and together they wept and prayed. But Mamie Till Bradley decided to make her lament public.[15] "As I stood and looked down under the glass covering of the casket, I said to myself over and over, 'There's my heart underneath that glass,'" she later told the *Chicago Defender*, "I wanted people to see what hatred of a human being, just because of the color of skin, can do."[16] As she grieved, she told her story and made the world listen; she showed her son's body and made the world look.

The casket sat open at the wake at A.A. Raynor & Sons Funeral home. There, for all to confront was the disfigured, waxy face, the hollowness on the back of the head, the evidence of white supremacy's violence to a child. Over 5,000 came to see.[17] The South Side of Chicago was a tight-knit community, and friends and neighbors came to lament alongside Mamie Till Bradley, sobbing and wailing, dressed in a sharp black suit and black pillbox hat, elegant even with her face pinched in pain. In fact, so many people came to the visitation that the funeral the next day had to be moved to the nearby Roberts Temple Church of God, a Pentecostal church on South State Street, where Sister Rosetta Tharpe had once played. Every pew was packed for the service. An estimated 10,000 people stood outside the church to listen on loudspeakers. And more came. Over the next several days, over 100,000 mourners filed through the church past the slain Emmett Louis Till before his body was finally put to rest.[18] "People were interested," Mamie explained later, "They wanted to know what was happening. One would go out and tell another and [they] looked at Emmett Louis (Bobo) Till."[19] And though it was painful to have her son on display, she welcomed them. "I would like for as many people to walk in here and see this thing as want to come," she said. "As long as we cover these things up, they're going to keep on happening . . . I'm pulling the lid off of this one."[20]

When coverage of Emmett Till's murder and accompanying photos ran in JET magazine on September 15 even more heard and saw and grieved. Underneath the gruesome visual, a caption read: "Close up of lynch victim bares mute evidence of horrible slaying . . . mutilated face of victim was left untouched by mortician at mother's request. She said she wanted 'all the world' to witness the atrocity."[21] All the world did.

"I was coming home from school the evening I heard about Emmett Till's death," Mississippi activist Anne Moody remembered, "Before I had known the fear of hunger, hell and the Devil But now there was a new fear . . . the fear of being killed just because I was black." Margaret Block, of Cleveland, Mississippi, had a similar experience. "I remember not being able to sleep when I saw [the photos]," she said. "Can you imagine being 11 years old and seeing something like that for the first time in your life and it being close to home?"[22] Many later footsoldiers and leaders in the Black freedom movement recalled seeing photos of Till as a catalyzing moment. Civil rights scholar David Halberstam has argued that this was "the first great media event of the civil rights movement."[23] "The death of Emmett Till touched us, it touched everybody, Block continued, "And we always said if we ever got a chance to do something, we were going to change things around here." The late Congressman John Lewis stated that Till's death "galvanized the country." "A lot of us young black students in the South," he said, "later on, we weren't just sitting in for ourselves—we were sitting in for Emmett Till."[24]

Mamie Till Bradley did not know all that was to come, but she did feel a sacred obligation to lament by speaking out. Less than five weeks after the trial ended in a not guilty verdict for J. W. Milam and Roy Bryant, on October 29, 1955, she addressed a standing room-only crowd at a Baltimore NAACP rally held at Bethel AME Church. She began her address, "I Want You to Know What They Did to My Boy," this way: "During the last two months, I have found it very necessary to talk to God quite a few times."[25] She described her anguish. "If I should even cry the rest of my life there wouldn't be enough tears for Emmett Till," she told those gathered, he "was just an ordinary boy like your ordinary boys and girls you have here."[26] She described being "overcome with grief" when she first went to Mississippi and saw her son. "To think that I had sent a fine fourteen-year-old boy to Money, Mississippi, to spend an innocent two weeks vacation and at the end of seven days, he came back to me in a pine box. That was enough to make anybody cry."[27] But she also described her sense of purpose.

"I have invested a son in freedom and I'm determined that his death isn't in vain," Mamie Till Bradley explained, turning theological. "When I was talking to God and pleading with Him and asking why did You let it be my boy, it was as if He spoke to me and said, 'Without the shedding of innocent blood, no cause is won.'"[28] This is a feature of Black lament. A sense of God's identification with suffering. The suffering servant, the Father who sends the son to the cross. And so she had prayed, "Lord, you gave your only son to remedy a condition, but who knows, but what the death of my only son might bring an end to lynching."[29] She continued, telling the crowd how this prayer transformed her lament: "I turned around then and thanked God that He felt that I was worthy to have a son that was worthy to die for such a worthy cause." The notion that the God of resurrection might use her grief to bring freedom comforted her. So did His presence. "The answer always comes back to me that there is a God up there. He's looking down here," she said, "I think God's looking out after me."[30] She concluded by offering hope to those gathered, just months after losing her only child: "The day is gone that we're nobodies; we are all somebodies, and together, I can't tell you how great we are as somebodies."[31]

Like John Lewis and Anne Moody, James Chaney had heard about Emmett Till. The Meridian, Mississippi native was twelve when the photos ran in *JET*. Though he could not have imagined that he would meet the same fate less than ten years later, Chaney likely felt a wave of sickening recognition at the white supremacist violence of his home state.[32] He also dedicated himself to changing it.

In 1959, after several years attending St. Joseph's Catholic School, Chaney transferred to the segregated public high school, T.J. Harris High. There, he and some classmates began wearing buttons showing their support of the local NAACP chapter, an action that announced Chaney as a young activist and also got him temporarily suspended. Nevertheless, he continued working with the NAACP Youth Council for several years and in 1963 connected with activists from the Congress of Racial Equality (CORE) who had come to Meridian. These included Michael "Mickey" and Rita Schwerner. Together, they worked to establish Freedom Schools (mostly in local Black churches), organize mass meetings, and lay the groundwork for a state-wide civil rights effort the following year.

In 1964, CORE joined with the Student Nonviolent Coordinating Committee (SNCC) and other groups to form the Council of Federated Organizations (COFO) and organize a massive voter registration drive in Mississippi. In what became known as "Freedom Summer," hundreds of college students, mostly white, volunteered to help canvas and register voters, organize political campaigns and mass meetings, and embody change by living and working alongside Black Southerners. Though full of youthful, heady exuberance, the Black and white volunteers, including James Chaney, were warned of the dangers of the undertaking. At the training in Oxford, Ohio, for instance, distributed pamphlets cautioned the "doors of cars should be locked at all times," "gas tanks must have locks," "No one should go anywhere alone, but certainly not in an automobile, and certainly not at night," and that "travel at night should be avoided unless absolutely necessary."[33] In fact, at that same training, Schwerner and Chaney got news from Mississippi that Mt. Zion Methodist, a church in Neshoba County that had hosted a Freedom School, had been burned to the ground and its members harassed in retaliation. It was a fiery reminder of the deranged determination of some white Mississippians to protect the white supremacist system. It was also a trap.[34]

Once back in Mississippi, Chaney and Schwerner took a new volunteer, Andrew Goodman, with them to investigate what happened at Mt. Zion. Leaving the church in a blue Ford station wagon, the three civil rights workers were detained by police, for some purported automotive infraction, and taken to the Neshoba County jail in Philadelphia, Mississippi. Local Klansmen alerted, Chaney, Schwerner and Goodman were released only to be immediately kidnapped and murdered. It was the first official day of Freedom Summer: June 21, 1964.

The disappearance of Chaney, Schwerner, and Goodman terrorized the community, cast a pall over their important work, and showed the violent resolve of many white Mississippians to uphold racial caste. For James Chaney's family, his mother Fannie Lee, father Ben, sisters Barbara, Julia, Janice, and little brother Ben, it was a more personal devastation. As Fannie Lee simply put it, "J. E.," as she called her son, left one day and "never came back." The family was harassed, with eggs and gunshot spraying the house, and death threats phoned in day and night. "They said they were going to put dynamite under my house," Fannie Lee recalled of the riled segregationists, "and blow us to bits."[35]

Forty-four days and a federal investigation later, the bodies of Chaney, Goodman, and Schwerner were unearthed. David Spain, the doctor who performed the autopsy, wrote in his report that the injuries Chaney had suffered "could only be the result of an extremely severe beating with either a blunt instrument or chain" and that it was "impossible" to tell if death had come due to the beating or the bullet wounds. "In my extensive experience of 25 years as a Pathologist and a Medical Examiner," Spain declared, "I have never witnessed bones so severely shattered."[36] Nevertheless, the body was prepared for a funeral, held on August 7, 1964.

And so, we come to another graveside to listen to dirges for James Chaney, full of honest anger, our second feature of lament. On a warm Friday evening men in suits and women in dresses, hats, and birdcage veils somberly processed into the stone First Union Missionary church to the sounds of a piano. The service began with a prayer, a theological anchoring: "Oh God our help in ages past, our hope for years to come . . . Thou the creator of all mankind and the Judge of all men, Oh God, who comforts the hearts of all mankind . . . Bless this mother, the family who's here, in their bereavement . . . " Then, David Dennis of CORE, the Assistant program director of the Mississippi Summer Project, clad in a denim work shirt, stood to offer remarks.

"Sorry," he began, "but I'm not here to do the traditional thing that most of us do at such a gathering." "What I want to talk about is really what I really grieve about," he continued, light blue eyes sharp, "I don't grieve for Chaney because, in fact, I feel he lived a fuller life than many of us will ever live. I feel that he's gotten his freedom and we're still fighting for it." Amens called out, Dennis railed against "people who don't care, those who do care but don't have the guts enough to stand up for it, and people busy up in Washington and other places using my freedom and my life to play politics with." He called out the President, the Governor of Mississippi, the federal government during Reconstruction, those involved in the slave trade and even fellow Black Mississippians, cowed for too long, those who" come to this memorial here and say 'Oh, what a shame,' go back home and pray to the Lord as we've done for years, and go back to work in some white folks' kitchen tomorrow, and forget about the whole dang-blasted thing."[37]

Voice clipped with anger, Dennis gave full expression before God to the people's honest lament. "I'm getting sick and tired. I'm sick and tired of going to memorials. I'm sick and tired of going to funerals. I got a bit of vengeance in my heart tonight. And I'm sick and tired and I can't help but feel bitter, you see, deep down inside." He continued, "I'm not going to stand here and ask anybody in here not to be angry tonight. Yeah, we have love in our heart—we've had it for years and years in this country . . . " He trailed off, repeating, "I'm sick and tired of that." From the pews, a woman's voice called back to Dennis, "I am too!"[38]

Another woman sick and tired was Fannie Lee Chaney. About a week later she spoke to a group gathered in front of a charred Mt. Zion Methodist, the very church James had been visiting before his death. "Well, you all know that I am Mrs. Chaney, the mother of James Chaney," she intoned evenly, "You all know what my child has done. He was trying so hard and he had two fellows from New York . . . " "Did you all know they came here to help us?" she continued, voice rising, "They died for us. They died for us. Now, is we gonna let this be in vain? I can't let my child's work go in vain . . . that was my child. And Mickey and Andrew–they was mine too. And I don't want these children's work to be lost. They's gone–they was beaten, they was dogged. Now we gonna let all of that die? We gonna let that die? No sir, I'll never let my child's life go in vain. I wanna know if somebody's gonna help me." Voices cried out "yes!" "I said I wasn't gonna say nothin.' But I couldn't just stay here, stand up here, sit up here. I gotta say somethin.'" Mrs. Chaney went on, sharing her pain and frustration. "Don't let those children's life go in vain. They dead. Don't let their work die . . . You all don't know . . . It's hard. It's hard. But every time there is something about freedom–I go. I got to go . . . And here I am."[39]

In showing up, in voicing her anger in honest lament, Chaney insisted that God hears and cares. That is a sign of faith. As her son Ben Chaney Jr. later said of his mother and Dr. Carolyn Goodman, Andrew's mother, "They carried a hell of a burden for a long time. A hell of a burden—knowing that your sons were murdered and the murderers were out on the streets going free . . . Strong women . . . They were able to endure, and continued to have faith. They never lost faith."[40]

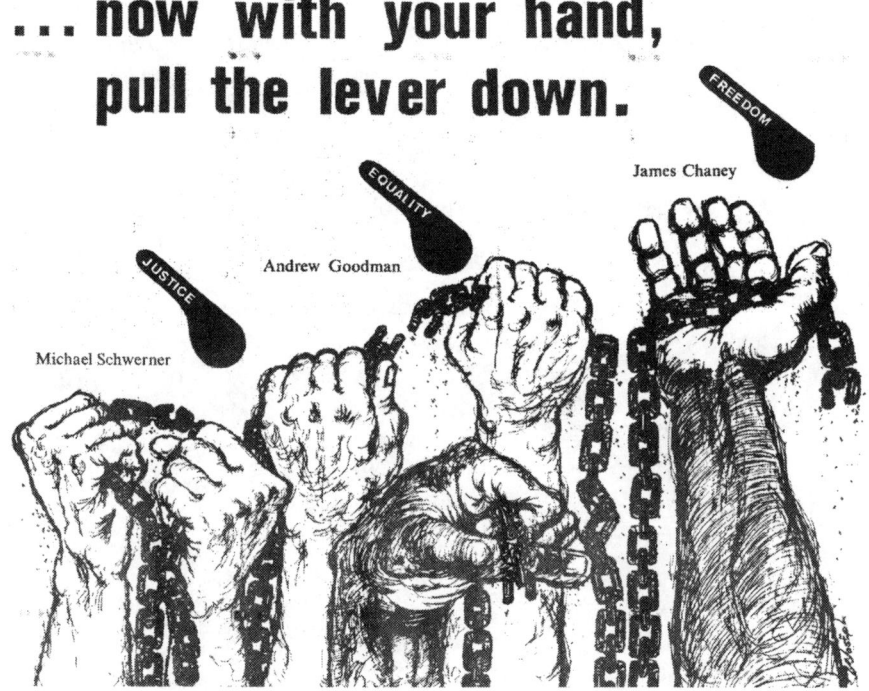

Figure 4.1. Page From Voting Pamphlet (Source: Wisconsin Historical Society)

About six months after Fannie Lou Chaney spoke in front of Mt. Zion Methodist Church in Neshoba County, there was another funeral held at another Zion Methodist Church, this one in Marion, Alabama. This time, it was to honor the murdered Jimmie Lee Jackson, a 26-year-old active in the local push for Black freedom.

A Marion native, Jackson was a military veteran who, upon returning from the service, lived with his family out in rural Perry County, working as a farmer and woodcutter. He was a deacon at St. James Baptist Church, the youngest in its history. It was through St. James' voter registration drive, as well as his own convictions about Christianity and democracy, that Jackson got involved with the Movement. He initially attempted to register to vote in Marion in 1962 but was repeatedly denied. This experience transformed him into a "devoted local organizer," who pressed for freedom and attended demonstrations.[41] One of these would cost him his life.

On February 18, 1965, Jimmie, his mother Viola, and his 82-year-old grandfather Cager Lee gathered with others in the community at Zion Methodist to protest the jailing of local SCLC leader James Orange. C.T Vivian offered remarks.[42] As they filed out of the church heading for the jail where Orange was being held, Alabama State troopers were waiting. They ordered them to disperse as all the street lights went out.[43] In the darkness and chaos, helmeted officers wielding guns and billy clubs chased and swung at the fleeing men and women. Jimmie, Viola, and Cager ducked into nearby Mack's Cafe, seeking safety, but officers pursued them, savagely beating those huddled inside. Hearing his mother's anguished voice, Jimmie Lee rushed toward her. He was then shot twice in the stomach by officer James Bonard Fowler. Despite what would be fatal injuries, Jackson gathered his shaken family and staggered out, officers continuing to bring their clubs down on his skull as they spilled onto the street. A bleeding Jackson was denied admission to Marion's local hospital and taken to Good Samaritan Hospital in Selma where, after telling his story to reporters and being served with an arrest warrant by State Police Colonel Al Lingo, he died eight days later.[44]

There were two funerals held for Jimmie Lee Jackson. The first, dubbed by SCLC organizers as a "freedom funeral," was held in Brown's Chapel in Selma.[45] Thousands of people packed the church, passing underneath a banner over the door that read: "Racism Killed Our Brother."[46] Inside, they listened to Rev. Ralph Abernathy describe Jackson's sacrifice, which he compared to the death of Abraham Lincoln, John Brown, Medgar Evers, and, tellingly for us, Emmett Till. They then traveled over to Marion for another service at Zion Methodist church, where Dr. King delivered remarks.[47] He described speaking with Jackson at his hospital bedside days earlier, "how radiantly he still responded, how he mentioned the freedom movement and how he talked about the faith that he still had in his God."[48] "Jimmie Lee Jackson is speaking to us from the casket," King said, gesturing to gleaming box draped in fronds and flowers below him, "he is saying to us that we must substitute courage for caution." Like David Dennis at James Chaney's funeral, King blamed local officials, federal politicians, and those upholding the status quo. And echoing the words of Fannie Lee Chaney and Mamie Till Bradley, he implored that Jackson's death not be in vain. Addressing the slain man local papers called an "obscure Negro farm hand," King promised in a hushed voice, "You died that we can vote, and we will vote."[49] This funeral dirge was also a statement of intent to act.

Lament involves naming what has been seen and done, it involves emotional honesty before God, but to lament rightly we must be compelled toward action. That is what happened in Alabama in 1965. Jimmie Lee Jackson's death served less as an occasion to show white supremacy's violences or reflect in anger, but to do something. Immediately after King finished speaking, he led 350 people past the lined state troopers, up to the Perry County courthouse to register to vote. Though Sheriff Jim Clark sought to obfuscate, two hundred applications were submitted.

And there would be more action in the coming days.[50] In an improvised dirge of his own the day of Jackson's death, the SCLC's James Bevel declared, "The blood of [Jimmie Lee] Jackson will be on our hands if we don't march. BE prepared to walk to Montgomery." With his characteristic intensity and ingenuity, he elaborated in the following days: "We will march Jimmie's body to the state capitol in Montgomery and lie it on the steps so Governor George Wallace can see what he's done."[51] It was this statement of action that formed the impetus for the Selma to Montgomery march that began a few days later with the infamous "Bloody Sunday" confrontation on the Edmund Pettus bridge, which, along with the murders of Rev. James Reeb and Mrs. Viola Liuzzo, brought a massive national outpouring of support and attention. Ultimately, these efforts in Alabama and the moral crisis they revealed persuaded President Lyndon Johnson to press Congress for the Voting Rights Act in a stunning speech in which he echoed the Movement itself, stating, "We Shall Overcome."

Cager Lee marched each time. Jackson's grandfather grieved with his feet. His lament propelled him to action. As Rabbi Abraham Joshua Heschel, who marched with alongside Lee toward Montgomery, would put it, "they were praying with their feet." They were lamenting with their feet too, every step taking them closer to the Kingdom.

But it's a long journey yet. The funeral dirges continue.

As I was writing this, I heard two pieces of news. The first was that the Leflore County Grand Jury, after discovering a decades old search warrant, declined to indict Carolyn Bryant [Donham], the white woman whose accusation of Emmett Till led to his lynching. Despite the fact that her husband and brother-in-law admitted to the murder decades ago, no one has ever been brought to justice. And it appears no one ever will be. It's worth noting, too, that of those convicted of the conspiracy to kill James Chaney, Andrew

Goodman and Mickey Schwerner, none served more than six years. The murderer of Jimmie Lee Jackson wasn't charged until 2007. The police officer convicted of killing him served a mere six months.

I also heard news that the murderers of Ahmaud Arbery were sentenced to additional life sentences, found guilty of federal hate crimes.[52] The vigilante racists who chased the jogging 25-year-old and killed him might never have been prosecuted been had it not been for a leaked video and the persistence of Black people who loved Ahmaud and understood that his life mattered. As Ahmaud's mother, Wanda Cooper Jones said, addressing the DOJ, "I'm very thankful that you guys brought these charges of hate crimes. But . . . you guys accepted a plea deal with these murderers who took my son's life." She continued, "Marcus and two of Ahmaud's aunties stood before the court and begged the judge not to take a plea deal that the DOJ [had asked for]." She herself did the same. "I begged them," she said, with notable anger. "That's not justice for Ahmaud. What we got today we wouldn't have got today if it wasn't for the fight the family put up. . . . what the DOJ did today, they was made to do." As this news came across the radio waves, I was reminded again, painfully, that the Black freedom struggle is ongoing. Carolyn Bryant is still alive. Ahmaud Arbery is still dead. There remains a struggle for justice. There remains cause to lament.

And yet, the lament, in all its screaming pain, in all its unflinching honesty, is an act of hope and ultimately of faith. "True reconciliation, justice and shalom," Rah explains, "require a remembering of suffering, an unearthing of shameful history and a willingness to enter into lament."[53] And so we must, drawing inspiration from the tradition of Black lament in the civil rights era. We lament with Mamie Till Bradley, who wanted the world to see her slain son because she knew a God who sees. We lament with Fannie Lee Chaney who expressed her honest anger because she had a God who hears. And we must lament with Cager Lee who marched because he believed God Incarnate walked among us. We must lament and keep showing, speaking, and walking toward true justice and beloved community.

BIBLIOGRAPHY

Arnold, Johann Christop. "Selma, 1965: The Unforgettable Funeral of Jimmie Lee Jackson." *Plough*, January 15, 2015.

Chaney Memorial, August 7, 1964. https://americanarchive.org/catalog/cpb-aacip_28-m901z42919.

"Civil Rights: Eulogy for a Woodchopper." *Time*, March 12, 1965.

"Emmett Till and the Impact of Images." Morning Edition, National Public Radio, June 23, 2004. https://www.npr.org/2004/06/23/1969702/emmett-till-and-the-impact-of-images.

"Father and son sentenced to life for a hate crime in Ahmaud Arbery's death." National Public Radio, August 8, 2022. https://www.npr.org/2022/08/08/1116261783/mcmichael-bryan-sentencing-ahmaud-arbery.

"Federal Judge Sentences Three Men Convicted of Racially Motivated Hate Crimes in Connection with the Killing of Ahmaud Arbery in Georgia." Department of Justice, August 8, 2022.

Halberstam, David. *The Fifties*. New York: Villard Books, 1993.

"History." Robert Temple Church of God. https://www.preserverobertstemple.com/history.

Houck, David and David Dixon, eds. *Women in the Civil Rights Movement*. Jackson: University Press of Mississippi, 2009.

"Jackson, Jimmie Lee." The Martin Luther King Jr. Institute for Research and Education (MMFR), Stanford University. https://kinginstitute.stanford.edu/encyclopedia/jackson-jimmie-lee.

"James Earl Chaney." *Mississippi Encyclopedia*. https://mississippiencyclopedia.org/entries/chaney-james-earl/.

Jones, Ryan M. "Who Mourns for Jimmie Lee Jackson?" National Civil Rights Museum. https://www.civilrightsmuseum.org/news/posts/who-mourns-for-jimmie-lee-jackson.

King, Martin Luther, Jr. Eulogy for Jimmie Lee Jackson, March 3, 1965, MMFR. https://kinginstitute.stanford.edu/encyclopedia/jackson-jimmie-lee.

Mendelsohn, Jack. *The Martyrs: Sixteen Who Gave their Lives for Racial Justice*. New York: Harper & Row, 1966.

Metress, Christopher, ed. *The Lynching of Emmett Till: A Documentary Narrative*. Charlottesville: University of Virginia Press, 2002.

Mitchell, Jerry. "Carolyn Bryant lied about Emmett Till. Did author Tim Tyson lie too?" *Mississippi Center for Investigative Reporting*, January 10, 2021.

Moody, Anne. *Coming of Age in Mississippi*. Delta Trade, 1968.

"Nation Horrified by Murder." *JET*, September 15, 1955, 6–9.

O'Connor, Kathleen. *Lamentation and the Tears of the World*. Maryknoll, NY: Orbis Books, 2002.

Postmortem Examination of James Chaney by Dr. David Spain, August 7, 1964. Veterans of the Civil Rights Movement. https://www.crmvet.org/docs/6408_chaney_spain.pdf.

Rah, Soon-Chan. *Prophetic Lament: A Call for Justice in Troubled Times*. Downers Grove, IL: InterVarsity Press, 2015.

Schwerner-Chaney-Goodman Memorial Service, August 16, 1964. Veterans of the Civil Rights Movement. https://www.crmvet.org/info/6408_chaney_memorial.pdf.

"The Murder of Emmett Till." Primary Sources, PBS. http://www.shoppbs.pbs.org/wgbh/amex/till/filmmore/ps_letters.html.

Till-Mobley, Mamie and Christopher Benson. *Death of Innocence: The Story of the Hate Crime that Changed America*. New York: Ballantine Books, 2003.

Whitfield, Stephen J. *A Death in the Delta*. Baltimore: John Hopkins Press, 1991.
Wisconsin Historical Society. "Security Handbook." Gabriner Papers Image 147189, MSS 575 Box 9 Folder 9. https://www.wisconsinhistory.org/Records/Image/IM147189.

NOTES

1. Soon-Chan Rah, *Prophetic Lament: A Call for Justice in Troubled Times* (Downers Grove, IL: InterVarsity Press, 2015), 22.
2. Rah, *Prophetic Lament*, 45.
3. Rah, *Prophetic Lament*, 44.
4. Kathleen O'Connor, *Lamentation and the Tears of the World* (Maryknoll, NY: Orbis Books, 2002), 19–20, quoted in Rah, Chapter 2.
5. Rah, *Prophetic Lament*, 50.
6. Rah, *Prophetic Lament*, 46.
7. Rah, *Prophetic Lament*, 47–48.
8. There is some danger here that we inadvertently sacralize historical Black suffering. It is not a spectacle for observation, nor does it provide any absolution. Even as we lament, Rah cautions, "lament is not simply the expression of sorrow in order to assuage feelings of guilt and the burden of responsibility." (206) We must be cautious to observe respectfully and responsibly.
9. Rah, *Prophetic Lament*, 54.
10. Rah, *Prophetic Lament*, 60.
11. Letter from Emmett Till to Mamie Till, undated, 1955, "The Murder of Emmett Till," Primary Sources, PBS, http://www.shoppbs.pbs.org/wgbh/amex/till/filmmore/ps_letters.html.
12. Jerry Mitchell, "Carolyn Bryant lied about Emmett Till. Did author Tim Tyson lie too?" *Mississippi Center for Investigative Reporting*, January 10, 2021.
13. "Two White Men Charged with Kidnapping Negro," *Delta Democrat-Times*, August 30, 1955.
14. Stephen J. Whitfield, *A Death in the Delta* (Baltimore: John Hopkins Press, 1991).
15. David Houck and David Dixon, eds., *Women in the Civil Rights Movement* (Jackson: University Press of Mississippi, 2009), 18.
16. "Mamie Bradley's Untold Story," *Chicago Defender*, April-June 1956.
17. Mamie Till-Mobley and Christopher Benson, *Death of Innocence: The Story of the Hate Crime that Changed America* (New York: Ballantine Books, 2003), 140.
18. Estimations vary. "Thousands Attend Funeral of Negro Boy Slain in South," *Jacksonville Daily Journal*, September 4, 1955; "Bury Slain Boy," *Chicago Tribune*, September 7, 1955; "History," Robert Temple Church of God, https://www.preserverobertstemple.com/history. It is perhaps worth mentioning that not all respected Mamie Till Bradley's decision. A Jackson, Mississippi newspaper denounced what they dubbed "paid agitator seeking to incite racial friction," calling the solemn memorial for Emmett Till a "carefully staged Congo circus at a Chicago

funeral home where a youngster's last rites were used as an occasion to collect funds for promoting further racial strife and perhaps fatten the wallets of agitators." Tom Ethridge, *Jackson Daily News*, September 11, 1955, in *The Lynching of Emmett Till: A Documentary Narrative*, ed. Christopher Metress (Charlottesville: University of Virginia Press, 2002), 41.

19. *Women*, 24.
20. *Women*, 24.
21. "Nation Horrified by Murder," *JET*, September 15, 1955, 6–9.
22. Anne Moody, *Coming of Age in Mississippi*, (Delta Trade, 1968), 127, 132, 136; "Emmett Till and the Impact of Images," Morning Edition, National Public Radio, June 23, 2004, https://www.npr.org/2004/06/23/1969702/emmett-till-and-the-impact-of-images.
23. David Halberstam, *The Fifties* (New York: Villard Books, 1993), 437.
24. Metress, *The Lynching of Emmett Till*, 3; See Whitfield, *A Death in the Delta*, 89–100.
25. *Women*, 18.
26. *Women*, 21.
27. *Women*, 22.
28. *Women*, 26.
29. *Chicago Defender*, September 10, 1955.
30. *Women*, 26.
31. *Women*, 26–27.
32. Several of Chaney's relatives, namely his father's cousin, J. Griggs, and his mother's step-grandfather, James Chapel, had financial altercations with white men in Mississippi after which they disappeared, presumed killed. For more, see: Michele Grigsby Coffey, "James Earl Chaney," *Mississippi Encyclopedia*, https://mississippiencyclopedia.org/entries/chaney-james-earl/.
33. Wisconsin Historical Society, "Security Handbook," Gabriner Papers Image 147189, MSS 575 Box 9 Folder 9, https://www.wisconsinhistory.org/Records/Image/IM147189.
34. Coffey, "James Earl Chaney."
35. "Fannie Lee Chaney, 84, Mother of Slain Civil Rights Worker, Is Dead," *The New York Times*, May 24, 2007.
36. Postmortem Examination of James Chaney by Dr. David Spain, August 7, 1964, Veterans of the Civil Rights Movement, https://www.crmvet.org/docs/6408_chaney_spain.pdf.
37. Chaney Memorial, August 7, 1964. Full audio here: https://americanarchive.org/catalog/cpb-aacip_28-m901z42919.
38. Chaney Memorial.
39. Schwerner-Chaney-Goodman Memorial Service, August 16, 1964, Veterans of the Civil Rights Movement, https://www.crmvet.org/info/6408_chaney_memorial.pdf.
40. Clyde Haberman, "A Life of Protest and Forgiveness," *The New York Times*, August 21, 2007.
41. Smith, *To Serve the Living*, 174.

42. "Jackson, Jimmie Lee," The Martin Luther King Jr. Institute for Research and Education (MMFR), Stanford University, https://kinginstitute.stanford.edu/encyclopedia/jackson-jimmie-lee.

43. Smith, *To Serve the Living*, 175.

44. Johann Christop Arnold, "Selma, 1965: The Unforgettable Funeral of Jimmie Lee Jackson," *Plough*, January 15, 2015. There is actually some dispute too about whether or not Jackson might have survived had not the hospital advised a second surgery. See Ryan M. Jones, "Who Mourns for Jimmie Lee Jackson?" National Civil Rights Museum, https://www.civilrightsmuseum.org/news/posts/who-mourns-for-jimmie-lee-jackson.

45. Smith, *To Serve the Living*, 175.

46. Smith, *To Serve the Living*, 176. Interestingly, Malcolm X, in his first visit to one of SNCC's nonviolent projects, had spoken at Brown's Chapel the previous month, on February 3, 1965, just weeks before his own murder later that month.

47. "Civil Rights: Eulogy for a Woodchopper," *Time*, March 12, 1965.

48. King, Eulogy for Jimmie Lee Jackson, March 3, 1965, MMFR, https://kinginstitute.stanford.edu/encyclopedia/jackson-jimmie-lee.

49. Jack Mendelsohn, *The Martyrs: Sixteen Who Gave their Lives for Racial Justice* (New York: Harper & Row, 1966), 133–35; Smith, *To Serve the Living*, 177.

50. "Civil Rights: Eulogy for a Woodchopper."

51. Jones, "Who Mourns for Jimmie Lee Jackson?" This quote might be apocryphal.

52. "Federal Judge Sentences Three Men Convicted of Racially Motivated Hate Crimes in Connection with the Killing of Ahmaud Arbery in Georgia," Department of Justice, August 8, 2022; "Father and son sentenced to life for a hate crime in Ahmaud Arbery's death," NPR, August 8, 2022, https://www.npr.org/2022/08/08/1116261783/mcmichael-bryan-sentencing-ahmaud-arbery.

53. Rah, *Prophetic Lament*, 58.

Chapter Five

"A Tribute in Tears and a Thrust for Freedom"

Medgar Evers and the Politics of Lament

Patrick L. Connelly

Jackson, Mississippi simmered with tension in the aftermath of the June 12, 1963 murder of Medgar Evers. In his role as Mississippi's first NAACP field secretary, Evers received significant public attention in the months prior to his death due to his fearless leadership within an expanding Jackson campaign against racial discrimination and segregation. Extensive media coverage also brought an increase in threats, something Evers and his family had already reckoned with for years but did so with heightened awareness in the final weeks of his life. On May 29, a Molotov cocktail was thrown into the same carport where, two weeks later, Evers would be shot from a distance by white supremacist Byron de la Beckwith after returning home from an NAACP mass meeting at New Jerusalem Baptist Church. Several days after Evers's assassination, thousands of mourners packed the Masonic Temple—a site that housed his office and where he had been present at many public gatherings—for his funeral. Myrlie Evers recalled in her memoir how the scale and design of the occasion had overtaken her personal wishes: "I wanted to get up and announce that there would be no funeral and that everyone could leave." But she was resigned to the fact that she "had shared my husband's life with the rest of the world, and I was going to share his death as well."[1]

Myrlie Evers's observation underscores how the rituals of mourning and lament can transcend the private grief of loved ones. Their public nature and function becomes particularly evident when examining the deadly violence inflicted upon activists in the Black freedom struggle. Memorial services, vigils, and mass meetings in honor of Medgar Evers were held not just in Mississippi or across the South, but throughout the nation. His death not only triggered a public outpouring of grief and outrage but a set of religiously infused practices that served to contextualize and compel political action in response. The language of martyrdom cast a large shadow over proceedings, as mourners frequently sought to understand the death of Evers as replete with meaning—with some even speaking in terms of his redemptive sacrifice.[2] This chapter will examine three public events where Evers was mourned and memorialized in the week following his death: the June 13 mass meeting held at Pearl Street A.M.E. Church in Jackson, the June 15 funeral held at Jackson's Masonic Temple, and the June 19 burial at Arlington National Cemetery in Washington. While these events had their own unique elements, they each shared a rejection of passive acquiescence to injustice and connected mourning to political action. The "tribute in tears," in the words of one observer of Evers's funeral, was also a "thrust for freedom."[3]

Less than twenty-four hours after Evers was murdered, a large crowd gathered at Pearl Street African Methodist Episcopal Church in Jackson on Wednesday evening, June 12, 1963. The original purpose of the mass meeting was not only to grieve the murder of Evers, but to organize a night march that NAACP officials ultimately canceled for several reasons. One was what had already occurred earlier in the day. *Chicago Daily News* reporter Raymond R. Coffey remarked that the service was the culmination of a day filled with rising tensions ("higher and hotter than the Mississippi sun") and "mourning marches" in Jackson, which led to over 100 arrests.[4] John R. Salter Jr., a white Tougaloo professor, civil rights activist, and Evers friend, recalled that a group of ministers arrested earlier in the day, since released, felt it was too dangerous. It was also rumored to be a "strong possibility" that Myrlie Evers may appear at the mass meeting and Salter suggested there was hesitation at the prospect of "upsetting her even further."[5] Coffey contrasted the atmosphere at Pearl Street A.M.E. with "the stirring, singing, handclapping mass meeting" he recently observed in Birmingham, AL prior to marches against segregation there. In Jackson, the mood "was one of quiet, solemn grief," with some in the audience wearing "black mourning armbands."[6] Salter noted, however, that while the service was "moving," there was a more "militant" tone: "There was anger in the faces of the people in the rows of pews, and there was anger in the speeches."[7] While Coffey surmised that one reason Black leaders called for the meeting was concern over the prospect of violence, it was also clear from his own reporting that public expressions of lament were to channel grief into action. "I hope you're going to do something more than say Amen," W.C. Patton, NAACP Director of Voter Education, told the crowd. Farish St. Baptist Church minister S. Leon Whitney implored that violence be rejected "for God's sake and for the sake of this movement." But he also specifically challenged them to continue the boycott initiatives that Evers had helped to organize.[8]

Another theme among mass meeting speakers was that the murder of Evers would not succeed in stemming the tide of freedom. Whitney decried the cowardice of the assassin and condemned the murder as an act of failure. "Bullets do not destroy ideas," he asserted. "Nothing destroys an idea but a better idea. And the best idea is freedom. That is what he [Evers] was fighting for." Reverend A.L. Johnson, a civil rights leader and Methodist minister in Jackson, concurred with Whitney and described the death of Evers as the "price of love for humanity." Ultimately, this egregious act of violence was not the end but a beginning: "His death is not a dead-end street but a new highway to hope."[9]

The dramatic climax of the Pearl Street A.M.E. meeting came when Myrlie Evers walked to the pulpit. She reminded the audience that she alone knew the degree of Medgar's sacrifices prior to his death and now faced the loss of a husband and a father to her children. Myrlie Evers implored the audience, "We cannot let his death be in vain." She hoped that many would "by his death, be able to draw some of his strength, some of his courage, and some of his determination to finish this fight." Her speech not only laid down a marker about the vital role she would play in securing the legacy of Medgar Evers but sought to channel public grief into fulfilling her late husband's tangible objectives of racial justice.[10] Indeed, Salter wrote that after the service concluded with an emotional singing of "We Shall Overcome," it was clear that "the Jackson movement was now rolling along with the greatest intensity." Those once hesitant were now "bursting through the rigid walls of fear" and embracing "large-scale direct action."[11]

Debates over direct action continued among national NAACP officials, Kennedy administration officials, and those on the ground in Jackson.[12] It was agreed that a march after the funeral of Evers would follow a prescribed route and protocols agreed upon by Jackson city officials and a group of Black clergymen. But it was evident to Salter and other supporters of mass demonstrations and civil disobedience that events were moving in their direction on the eve of the funeral.[13] Two days after Myrlie Evers's dramatic Pearl Street address, a packed house of over four thousand attended the funeral of Medgar Evers at the sweltering Masonic Temple in Jackson. Dignitaries in attendance included civil rights leaders and activists such as Martin Luther King, Ralph Abernathy, Roy Wilkins, Ralph Bunche, James Meredith, and Dick Gregory. Similar to the Pearl Street A.M.E. mass meeting, the funeral embodied a public form of grief and lament that provided an impetus for action—as became apparent immediately after the service ended.

One detailed account of the memorial service comes from James E. Jackson, a Black civil rights and labor activist, member of the Communist Party, and editor of the periodical *The Worker* who published his observations in a pamphlet titled, "At the Funeral of Medgar Evers in Jackson Mississippi: A Tribute in Tears and a Thrust for Freedom." The first speaker was Dr. T.R.M. Howard, who gave Evers his first job after college selling insurance in Mount Bayou, Mississippi and stirred his interest in getting involved in the NAACP. Despite Jackson's description of Howard's remarks as a "secular tribute," Howard also "invoked the Biblical quotation that 'without the shedding of blood there can be no remission of sins.'" He served notice that Black Mississippians were tired of turning the other cheek: "Our neck has gotten tired of turning now!" Jackson documented "a great roar of shouted approvals from the mourners." Howard likened Evers to John Brown and called for 50,000 Black citizens to join the NAACP within a month.[14] NAACP Executive Secretary Roy Wilkins also spoke, offering a powerful rebuke of the racist structures that put Evers's assassin "behind that rifle." He insisted that this act and the systemic white supremacy that fueled it were in vain. "Medgar Evers," Wilkins contended, "was the symbol of our victory and of their defeat." His life symbolized the "threat to the system" and his assassination would only hasten its demise. "They can fiddle and they can throw a few more victims to the lions," Wilkins concluded, "but Rome is burning and a new day is over yonder."[15]

Local ministers also participated in the service, including a eulogy given by the family's minister, G.C. Hunte. After the opening hymn, "Be Not Dismayed," Pearl Street A.M.E. minister G.R. Haughton—who had been arrested in a protest march two days earlier—gave the invocation. S. Leon Whitney of Farish Street Baptist Church read Scripture before the crowd sang "We Shall Overcome." Hunte, the minister of New Hope Baptist Church, where the Evers family were members, asserted that "Medgar laid down his life for his friends." The mourners responded with "Amens" before he added, "It's for you to decide whether he died in vain."[16] Hunte made clear to the Evers family, however, that his death was not meaningless. "Your father died that you might live in a better world than he did," he assured them.[17] Charles Evers recalled that the eulogies of his brother carried the same song in different keys: Medgar Evers had repudiated hatred of his white enemies. "He used to hate the whites almost as bad as I did," Charles Evers mused, "but I realized at his funeral that the night he was killed, Medgar Evers did not hate anyone."[18] Civil rights activist and fellow NAACP leader Aaron Henry of Clarksdale, MS later remembered how the service ended with "This May be the Last Time," a "sad hymn" tinged with themes of mortality, death, and the life beyond.[19]

Myrlie Evers nearly broke down as the casket was carried out of the temple, but she remained ambivalent about how the funeral had transpired. She recalled that her husband once said he preferred a short funeral, "no longer than a half hour," without any long eulogies. "When I'm gone, I'm gone," she remembered him saying, "and I won't know anything about it." Though not thrilled with the arrangements, Myrlie Evers marveled at certain aspects of what occurred that day beyond her private grief. She expressed astonishment not only at the size of the crowd at the Masonic Temple, but what happened afterward in the streets of Jackson. As the motorcade carried the casket to Collins Funeral Home, she recalled reaching "the bottom of a long sloping hill" and looking behind her to see a "mass of people" marching behind them. She took in the scene of an "unending parade of black faces" defiantly filling the road from curb to curb in a manner that would not have been allowed "while Medgar was alive and could have seen it." They sang as they marched, and Myrlie Evers recalled not only "We Shall Overcome" but "Oh Freedom," with its verse, "Before I'd be a slave, I'd be buried in my grave, and go home to my Lord and be free!" This "solid phalanx of mourners," as she described it, was full of those who once resisted NAACP involvement due to fears of losing jobs, of the elderly walking a mile and a half "under a blistering sun," and of younger Black citizens who felt increasing boldness as "sorrow turned to anger" when policemen lined up to stop the march.[20]

Aaron Henry, who rode with Myrlie Evers as she observed these things, noted that while tears flowed at the funeral, the crowd was "seething with sorrow" when they left the Masonic Temple. A tense standoff ensued once a predominantly Black group of marchers on Lynch Street met white police officers wielding nightsticks. National newspaper coverage of the day was often like the example of Nashville, Tennessee's *Tennessean*, which published the headline, "Jackson Police Quell Riot" with the subheading, "Officers Stoned by Irate Negroes." A picture of two Black men throwing rocks adorned the page.[21] Jackson's own *Clarion-Ledger*, notorious for its derisive coverage of civil rights activism, focused on "white-led agitation" (likely a reference to Salter and Tougaloo chaplain Edwin King) that provoked the unrest.[22]

James Jackson, John Salter, Myrlie Evers, and Aaron Henry saw events differently, however. Jackson referred to it as "a spontaneous demonstration of revolution" that broke out in the face of "brutal conditions" imposed by Mayor Allen C. Thompson, which include a failed prohibition on "singing or shouting any slogans." Jackson credited one little girl with initiating a round of "This Little Light of Mine." As the crowd moved across Capital Street and Farish Street intersection, the line of demarcation "between the two worlds" of Black and white Jacksonians, the police responded with brutality. Jackson's pamphlet recounted several stories of beaten demonstrators, "Rebel yells" let out by police officers, and dogs being used against marchers.

Despite this retaliation, James Jackson described the day as one that "began in sorrow and mourning for the martyr, Medgar Evers" but ended triumphantly. It unleashed "a tableau of poetic courage and a glorious manifestation of the unconquerable will of the Negro masses of the southland to gain the freedom goals for which Medgar Evers and so many others have given their lives."[23]

John R. Salter Jr. and Ed King also felt something was different that day. Salter recalled the dramatic moment when the song "Oh, Freedom" began to surge "softly and mournfully" through the crowds who had moved toward Collins Funeral Home. This song was followed by "This Little Light of Mine" with the ad-libbed lyrics, "All over Capitol Street, I'm going to let it shine." Salter watched as the crowd began to surge toward Capitol Street, continuing to sing and crying out, "We want Medgar's killer! We want freedom! Freedom! Freedom!" At this point, police who had amassed in large numbers responded in force. Salter and King were quickly arrested. Salter recalled being put in a paddy-wagon with others, including a bleeding man who had been struck with a club and a woman in tears with a ripped dress. Those arrested were then taken to the state fairgrounds, where Salter and King were accused by police of being instigators. Officers sought a reaction from the two activists that would allow them to respond in retribution. Even amidst the fears and frustrations of that day, Salter hailed what he called "the largest black protest in the history of Mississippi." Grassroots activists like Salter "had now reached a point where we could never, never turn back."[24]

Myrlie Evers's account also corroborated Jackson's pamphlet and Salter's experience regarding the violent response from police—details that were also confirmed by a *New York Times* report she cited. Evers described crowds being pushed back, Black marchers being "plucked from the crowd and hustled into waiting police vans," drawing of weapons, preparing fire hoses, and utilizing dogs. Incidents included demonstrators being struck by shotgun butts and women being clubbed. This show of violent force triggered a response, with some protesters throwing bricks, bottles and other items at police. Evers quoted Deputy Police Chief A.L. Ray, who addressed the crowd with a bullhorn and stated, "You came here to honor a dead man and you have brought dishonor." These words provoked outrage from the crowd, particularly from those "in their 20's and 30's," some of whom screamed and launched projectiles in response to police escalation. At this point, John Doar, a Justice Department official who later would serve as Assistant United States Attorney General for Civil Rights, stepped from the crowd into "the no-man's land of broken glass and stones." Doar called for calm and Evers credited him with defusing a situation that could have been much worse.[25]

Aaron Henry also praised Doar for providing the authoritative composure and words "like the Lord had spoken" that prevented a larger breakout of violence on that day. Yet, it is also evident from his account that like the marchers on that day, grief and lament fueled Henry's own sense of responsibility to act. Henry wrote that he stayed in Mississippi and remained in the movement because the sacrifices of people like Evers—and civil rights worker Andrew Goodman, whom Henry helped recruit to Mississippi—not to mention the "severe physical and economic reprisals" faced by thousands of others. "The only way I can do justice to them and others who made sacrifices is to remain in the movement and fight for what they believed in," Henry concluded.[26]

The galvanizing impact of the funeral and its aftermath was also evident at events surrounding the burial of Evers at Arlington National Cemetery. Evers was a World War II veteran whose experiences serving in England, France, and Belgium transformed his expectations of how life should be for himself and other Black citizens upon returning to Mississippi. After his death, the American Veterans Committee recommended to Myrlie Evers that his body be buried at Arlington. She initially resisted the idea. Myrlie and Medgar Evers had once purchased "a burial plot in a Negro cemetery," a mere ten-minute drive from their home, and always assumed they would be buried in Mississippi. Just as he had wished for a short, unpretentious funeral, he likely assumed a simple burial in the state he deeply loved and refused to leave, despite the injustices and danger it brought him. Myrlie Evers did finally give her consent to the Arlington burial, however, writing that in death just as in life, "he did not belong to me alone."[27] Here was another moment, in her process of grieving and lamenting the death of her husband, where the public purposes of mourning transcended private wishes. The body of Medgar Evers was taken by hearse from Collins Funeral Home in Jackson to Meridian, Mississippi, where a train "would carry him out of Mississippi forever," as Salter put it.[28] From Meridian, Medgar Evers's casket made its way to Washington DC, where hundreds of mourners met the train at Union Station and marched behind the hearse that carried him to a local funeral home. Handbills were given out with his picture and the words, "He sacrificed his life for you."[29]

During the two days before burial at Arlington on Wednesday, June 18, John Wesley African Methodist Episcopal Church hosted an open casket viewing. Charles Evers recalled that the church's minister E. Franklin Jackson had supported civil rights at a time when other Black churches hesitated to do so. Reverend Jackson had invited Medgar Evers to speak there a year earlier to a crowd of two hundred. "Now we opened his casket," Charles Evers continued, "and twenty-five thousand people paid their respects."[30] As Evers biographer Michael Vinson Williams observed, the long line of mourners coming to see the slain civil rights leader's body represented "all socioeconomic and political backgrounds, from district court judges to taxi cab drivers." The appearance of Nation of Islam members outside the church indicated that Evers "transcended religious boundaries" as well.[31] A 1963

Jet magazine report on the three-day mourning period in Washington made the case that one reason Evers appealed to so many was his advocacy for the common person—and especially the underprivileged. "Not a conferee in oak-paneled conference rooms or one given to high society functions," Medgar Evers fought for the people "in the poorest most underdeveloped rebel state in the union." He brought together "the impoverished, the rural, the religious" into a coalition for civil rights.[32]

"This last look at Evers" for many who passed through John Wesley A.M.E. Church was, as one newspaper report pointed out, "their first as well." Unknown to many mourners a week earlier, he was now "a part of their lives"—a development they were trying to understand. "I don't know him personally, of course" an unnamed woman was quoted as saying. "I just wanted to see this man who died trying to do something for my race." Another unnamed woman mused on the impact of seeing his body and finding meaning in his death: "I think now we're going to succeed. I think this is going to make the black people keep going until they get what they want." For Reverend Jackson, these sentiments only confirmed the decision to bury Evers in Washington. "It gives national significance to Evers' death," he stated. "If he had been buried in Mississippi, he'd have been soon forgotten." Choosing to publicly lament the death of Evers in the nation's capital "will awaken the sleeping conscience of people everywhere."[33]

The final stop for Evers's body was Arlington National Cemetery. As the procession of cars passed the Lincoln Memorial on the way to Arlington, Myrlie Evers recalled the pride she felt at seeing Medgar Evers not only as a husband and father but as "a great American being put to rest in a place with many other American heroes."[34] The interment of Evers at Arlington, as opposed to a more secluded burial in Mississippi, provided an opportunity to cast Evers in a larger national story. Linking Evers to Abraham Lincoln was an important element in doing so. However, the connection with Lincoln did not only happen after Evers was assassinated. A 1958 *Ebony* profile titled "Why I Live in Mississippi" demonstrated his local roots while introducing him to a national audience. It drew attention to a plaque Evers had on his living room wall with a quote attributed to Lincoln, one that spoke to Evers "in his own time of trouble" as he reflected upon the state of the civil rights fight in his home state and the threats he faced there. The plaque read, "I have been driven many times to my knees by the overwhelming conviction that I had nowhere else to go . . . My own wisdom, and that of all about me seemed insufficient for that day." The piece concluded with the observation that "the same 'overwhelming conviction' which sent Lincoln to his knees" led Evers "back to his Bible, his prayer, his God, and his knees, and has brought him back, each time, with renewed vigor to the battle he knows he was made for."

The Lincoln comparison was even more pronounced when *Ebony* decided to republish the piece in 1963, several months after Evers was murdered.[35]

Micki McElya notes in *The Politics of Mourning: Death and Honor in Arlington National Cemetery* that "overt and subtle comparisons to Lincoln" were also found within the memoir Myrlie Evers co-wrote with William Peters four years after the death of her husband. The title itself, *For Us, The Living*, is a phrase drawn from the Gettysburg Address and is meant to suggest an ongoing responsibility to complete the work advanced by those who gave their lives for it. McElya persuasively argues that throughout public expressions of mourning, media coverage, and his widow's memoir, references to Lincoln "reinforced the idea of Evers's martyrdom and drew a long line back to the enslaved and the Civil War in the struggle for black freedom."[36]

The national recasting of Evers was not only about his legacy but the hope that his death would not be in vain. An overflowing crowd heard African Methodist Episcopal Church Bishop and NAACP board chairman Stephen Gill Spottswood offer a reading of psalms, prayers, and a brief eulogy at Fort Myer Chapel on the grounds at Arlington. "I hope Medgar Evers will be the last black American to give his life in the struggle to make the Constitution come alive," Spottswood told the audience, who responded with "a chorus of amens."[37] As the audience moved to the gravesite, they heard from Mickey Levine of the American Veterans Committee and from Roy Wilkins. Levine emphasized Evers's heroism and insisted that the fight would continue: "We shall go to the Congress; we shall go to the people; he shall not have died in vain." Wilkins cast the occasion as a moment of reckoning for the nation. "Medgar Evers believed in his country," he said, but "it now remains to be seen whether his country believes in him."[38] As Myrlie Evers took in both the setting and the ceremony, she recalled feeling "a sense of pride in being a real American and not merely a second-class citizen."[39] As McElya astutely infers, the Arlington setting recast Evers as a national hero who embodied "honor and patriotism" while providing a "dissident script for national sacrifice," the impact of which would be felt far beyond the ceremony itself.[40]

The assassination of Medgar Evers was, at its core, a tragedy and travesty that came with a profound human cost. A native son of Mississippi was cut down in the prime of life as he tried to hold his state and country accountable to the ideals and institutions of American democracy. A woman and her children were deprived of a husband and father, taken from them in traumatic circumstances at their very home. Many across Jackson, the state of Mississippi, and the nation lost a friend, colleague, and advocate. Justice was not served to his killer for decades, which was evidence that the white supremacist system that Evers sought to dismantle persisted. Despite these realities, the events of public grief and lament in the week following his assassination bore witness to the strong desire that his death not be futile. The Pearl Street mass meeting, the funeral at the Masonic Temple, and the days of mourning that culminated in an Arlington National Cemetery burial were not just tributes in tears alone. They served to redeem his death as a catalyst for urgent, direct action to ensure the nation lived up to its promise of freedom and the rights of citizenship for all.

BIBLIOGRAPHY

Ditmer, John. *Local People: The Struggle for Civil Rights in Mississippi*. Urbana: University of Illinois Press, 1994.

Evers, Charles and Andrew Szanton. *Have No Fear: The Charles Evers Story*. New York: John Wiley & Sons, Inc., 1997.

Evers, Myrlie and William Peters. *For Us, the Living*. Garden City, NY: Doubleday & Company, Inc., 1967.

Henry, Aaron with Constance Curry. *Aaron Henry: The Fire Ever Burning*. Jackson: University Press of Mississippi, 2000.

Jackson, James E. "At the Funeral of Medgar Evers in Jackson, Mississippi: A Tribute in Tears and a Thrust for Freedom." New York: Publishers New Press, 1963. Collection of the Smithsonian National Museum of African American History and Culture, Gift of the family of Dr. Maurice Jackson and Laura Ginsburg. https://nmaahc.si.edu/object/nmaahc_2010.55.57.

McElya, Micki. *The Politics of Mourning: Death and Honor in Arlington National Cemetery*. Cambridge: Harvard University Press, 2016.

Nossiter, Adam. *Of Long Memory: Mississippi and the Murder of Medgar Evers*. Cambridge, MA: De Capo Press, 2002.

Salter Jr., John R. *Jackson, Mississippi: An American Chronicle of Struggle and Schism*. Lincoln: University of Nebraska Press, 2011.

Williams Michael Vinson. *Medgar Evers: Mississippi Martyr*. Fayetteville: University of Arkansas Press, 2011.

1. Myrlie Evers and William Peters, *For Us, the Living* (Garden City, NY: Doubleday & Company, Inc., 1967), 316.

2. The title of the most comprehensive monograph on the life and career of Evers is understandably subtitled, "Mississippi Martyr." See Michael Vinson Williams, *Medgar Evers: Mississippi Martyr* (Fayetteville: University of Arkansas Press, 2011). Adam Nossiter argues that turning Evers into a "martyr-symbol" who is "piously recalled in some public commemorations of the civil rights era" reduces Evers to a cliché and makes his assassination seem overly determined. See Adam Nossiter, *Of Long Memory: Mississippi and the Murder of Medgar Evers* (Cambridge, MA: De Capo Press, 2002), 26, 61.

3. James E. Jackson, "At the Funeral of Medgar Evers in Jackson, Mississippi: A Tribute in Tears and a Thrust for Freedom." (New York: Publishers New Press, 1963). Collection of the Smithsonian National Museum of African American History

and Culture, Gift of the family of Dr. Maurice Jackson and Laura Ginsburg, https://nmaahc.si.edu/object/nmaahc_2010.55.57.

4. Raymond R. Coffey, "Did He 'Die in Vain'? Widow of Slain Leader Exhorts Mass-Meeting Crowd," *The Huntsville (AL) Times*, June 13, 1963, 14.

5. John R. Salter Jr., *Jackson, Mississippi: An American Chronicle of Struggle and Schism* (Lincoln: University of Nebraska Press, 2011), 191. Note: An earlier edition of Salter's memoir was published in 1979.

6. Coffey, "Did He 'Die in Vain'?," 14.

7. Salter, *Jackson, Mississippi*, 192.

8. Coffey, "Did He 'Die in Vain'?," 14.

9. David Maddux, "Evers' widow speaks at rally," *The Chronicle (Pascagoula, MS)*, June 14, 1963, 5. Chronicling America: Historic American Newspapers, Library of Congress, https://chroniclingamerica.loc.gov/lccn/sn87065526/1963-06-14/ed-1/seg-5/.

10. Evers and Peters, *For Us, The Living*, 310, 311.

11. Salter, *Jackson, Mississippi*, 193.

12. John Ditmer argues that even during his lifetime, Evers had to deal with the tensions between what the national leaders of the NAACP desired, not to mention the Kennedy administration, and what his "basic combative instincts" would have wanted when it came to direct action tactics. He suggests that Evers "deserved—in his lifetime—the respect and support of the powerful people who later publicly identified themselves so closely with his cause." See Ditmer, *Local People: The Struggle for Civil Rights in Mississippi* (Urbana: University of Illinois Press, 1994), 169.

13. For an overview of the debates and dynamics leading up to the Evers funeral among NAACP officials, local activists, and tensions with the Southern Christian Leadership Conference, see Salter, *Jackson, Mississippi*, 202–8.

14. Jackson, "At the Funeral of Medgar Evers in Jackson Mississippi."

15. Jackson, "At the Funeral of Medgar Evers in Jackson Mississippi."

16. Relman Morin, "Evers Mourners Charge Police Barricades," *Philadelphia Inquirer*, June 16, 1963, 7. While newspaper accounts provided valuable details of the funeral itself, much of the coverage and headlines have to filtered through their often sensationalized focus on the possibility of violence in the aftermath, with Black protesters being portrayed as the primary instigators.

17. "Thousands Attend Evers Funeral, March 17 Blocks Behind Hearse," *The Mississippi Enterprise*, June 22, 1963, 1. Chronicling America: Historic American Newspapers, Library of Congress. https://chroniclingamerica.loc.gov/lccn/sn87065258/1963-06-22/ed-1/seq-1/.

18. Charles Evers and Andrew Szanton, *Have No Fear: The Charles Evers Story* (New York: John Wiley & Sons, Inc., 1997), 139.

19. Aaron Henry with Constance Curry, *Aaron Henry: The Fire Ever Burning* (Jackson: University Press of Mississippi, 2000), 150.

20. Evers and Peters, *For Us, The Living*, 315, 317, 318, 319.

21. This headline, similar to the previously referenced *Philadelphia Inquirer* article, drew from Relman Morin's Associated Press report from Jackson. See Morin,

"Jackson Police Quell Riot; Officers Stoned By Irate Negroes," *The Nashville Tennessean*, June 16, 1963, 1.

22. "Funeral March Finishes in White-Led Agitation," *The Clarion-Ledger* (Jackson, MS), June 16, 1963, 1.

23. Jackson, "At the Funeral of Medgar Evers in Jackson Mississippi."

24. Salter, *Jackson, Mississippi*, 213, 214, 216, 219.

25. Evers and Peters, *For Us, The Living*, 320, 321, 322.

26. Henry and Curry, *Aaron Henry*, 150, 151, 165.

27. Evers and Peters, *For Us, The Living*, 322.

28. Salter, *Jackson, Mississippi*, 223.

29. "500 March in Capital Behind Evers' Hearse," *Los Angeles Times*, June 18, 1963, 20.

30. Evers and Szanton, *Have No Fear*, 141.

31. Williams, *Medgar Evers*, 298–9.

32. Simeon Booker, "Medgar Evers Military Burial," *Jet* 24 no. 11 (July 4, 1963): 8.

33. Dickson Preston, "Endless Line Views Evers Before Burial," *The Evansville (Indiana) Press*, June 18, 1963, 4.

34. Evers and Peters, *For Us, The Living*, 324.

35. "Why I Live in Mississippi," *Ebony* 18 no. 11 (September 1963): 148.

36. Micki McElya, *The Politics of Mourning: Death and Honor in Arlington National Cemetery* (Cambridge: Harvard University Press, 2016): 239, 240.

37. Booker, "Medgar Evers Military Burial," 9.

38. Evers and Peters, *For Us, The Living*, 325, 326.

39. Evers and Peters, *For Us, The Living*, 326.

40. McElya, *The Politics of Mourning*, 239.

PART II

Lament and Historical Pedagogy

Chapter Six

The Psalms and the Historical Pedagogy of Lament

Timothy Fritz

The oak-lined lane of the stately southern home is perhaps at the forefront of many American's imaginations of Southern architecture. For some, it conjures memories of family beach trips, an afternoon at the golf course, or reunions with loved ones under the shady canopy. It is an enduring image that has adorned the covers of magazines and travel guides for almost a century. While some may recognize that this manufactured ecology of wealth has strong roots in the systematic oppression of slavery, the compartmentalization and commodification of these historical memories has resulted in an astonishing amount of tourism dollars. Unfortunately, recent movements seeking to merge the architecture, science, and history of the American plantation experience are sometimes met with vitriol by some visitors expecting to hear a happier story.

The most recent round of publicized resistance to the inclusion of enslaved experiences in historic sites took place in the South Carolina lowcountry. McLeod Plantation made national news after a negative online review went viral on Twitter. The Washington Post ran the story shortly after, thrusting negative visitor impressions of black experiences at plantation sites into the popular media for a few days.[1] Although such lackluster reviews were well in the minority, these negative comments underscored a thread of cognitive dissonance in American society. Many plantation sites now open to the public housed enslaved Africans who kept the grounds, produced crops of value, and provided the white residents a more manageable lifestyle than they would have otherwise enjoyed. In most cases, the enslaved residents on these properties outnumbered the free ones. While focusing on the enslaved population provides a fuller context of the human experience at these plantations,

American educational trends traditionally gloss over the brutality of chattel slavery in favor of some notion of romanticism to which many have attached themselves. When Middleton Place, a historical plantation site outside of Charleston, attempted to hold a Juneteenth celebration as part of ongoing efforts to balance their interpretation of the property in 2020, it was canceled due to threats against the safety of the staff and visitors.[2] Drayton Hall, a similar historic site just down the road from Middleton Place, also increased security around the same time. Rather than confront the idea of human suffering by celebrating the positive changes that ended slavery, some individuals threatened violence.

Historians, educators, and museum professionals share the challenge of creating a balanced history of a traumatic experience intended for large audiences. In addition to frequent politicization, the historical operation and enduring legacy of systematic oppression is difficult to explain in these settings, resulting in uneven learning outcomes and varied visitor experiences. The wrongs of the past cannot be addressed without acknowledging the historical pain and lingering effects of phenomena like slavery. Addressing these historical truths through the idea of lament is a valuable first step in helping an audience make sense of experiences that are at times very different from their own. In fact, the idea of lament thrust McLeod Plantation into a national conversation of the legacy of slavery and race relations in the United States following the racially motivated mass shooting a few miles away at Emanuel AME a few years earlier.[3]

In South Carolina, the June 2015 mass shooting at Emanuel AME Church was a catalyst for a renewed focus on the problematic parts of South Carolina's history. The nationwide process of lament led many to question the ideologies that led to such a violent act. In the aftermath, it was clear that local historic sites could play a pivotal role in educating the public and building a new shared memory of eighteenth and nineteenth-century America. In November 2019, McLeod Plantation Historic Site and Caw Caw Interpretive Center, both public sites managed by Charleston County Parks and Recreation, joined the International Coalition of Sites of Conscience, a network of over 300 public history sites in sixty-five countries, dedicated to lamenting and remembering historical events in a manner that leads to action and social justice in the present day.[4] Connecting the history of the past with the movement of the present also offers important models for universities to participate in the work of social justice and adapt in classroom settings when their communities need them to function as "sites of conscience" as well.

Institutions of higher education often operate within the whims of donors, trustees, and politicians. At times, there may only appear to be a narrow window to address traumatic issues of the past honestly. Surely the university should also be a site of conscience in its community. But like the troubled visitors to McLeod, specific work is required to lead students, staff, and surrounding residents through the process of lament. This chapter will offer practical reflections on applying biblical concepts of lament to university programming and cirriculum. As demonstrated in the Psalms, Biblical lament offers a renewed pedagogy of inclusivity from which the whole community benefits and learns. By looking at the value of corporate lament, its application in university settings, and how it influences desired outcomes, it argues that lament is a central factor in linking academic work to community renewal.

Whether at historical sites, in the movies, or the university classroom, there is often a clash between what the public expects to learn and the actual source material. Confronting new ideas, experiences, and points of view that force us to reconcile history with collective historical memory (defined here as that version of our history that informs our perceptions of belonging in society) is good thing. These crucial aspects of identity frequently arise in high school and college classrooms, often with conflicts that mirror those observed at historical sites dealing with the violent truths of human slavery. Public resistance to historic interpreters mirrors recent opposition to the greater inclusion of slavery and the African American experience at all levels of education in at least thirty-six states. Tennesee, for example, urges impartiality when addressing aspects of history ambiguously deemed controversial. Teaching resentment of any group of people, or suggesting that race places a role in oppression, is prohibited.[5] The identity battle is not confined to museums but is a more significant part of a decades-long American culture shift. Denise Hopkins recognized that beginning in the 1960s, the American Christian church's newfound focus on liturgy and eucharistic celebration resulted in themes of thanksgiving and victory replacing older themes of "contrition and penitence."[6] Soong-Chan Rah argues that the ensuing shift inspired an evangelical culture where "a triumphalistic theology of celebration and privilege rooted in a praise-only narrative is perpetuated by the absence of lament and the underlying narrative of suffering that informs lament."[7] Lament is essential in rebalancing both historical memory and cultural education. While Rah looks to the book of Lamentations as a lens to examine the present-day church's role in racial reconciliation, the corporate structure of the Psalms also provides a roadmap to recovering historical perspectives. Together, biblical lament offers a realistic view of historically oppressed people, strategies to address the injustice that remains, and structure to educate individuals on both.

Lament in Public Life

Lament is the acknowledgment of divine providence amid a seemingly hopeless situation. In the history of the United States, the capture, forced transport, and enslavement of Africans in the colonial and early republic eras, and the further enslavement and disenfranchisement of their descendents well into the twentieth century, encapsulated generations of lived experience with little end in sight. Until recently, as seen with historic sites, that experience was interpreted primarily through its final stages, with a focus on triumphant individuals and leaders who forged a way out of bondage and oppression and lived to tell about it. American history leans toward celebrating those who overcame trying times rather than those who never found respite. What do we make of ordinary people who struggled, hoped, but did not live to see significant change? America has trouble lamenting, and the problem spreads into our secular and sacred institutions. Christian inspired civic religion deals with hard times in American history by highlighting the power of faith and perseverance, but as Soong-Chan Rah notes, our churches struggle with balancing lament.[8] Research shows that many American churches, regardless of denomination, struggle to incorporate concepts of suffering within worship music and other aspects of liturgy, creating an environment where "the power of lament is minimized, and the underlying narrative of suffering that requires lament is lost."[9] Rah's observation that such liturgical practices cause congregations to forget the reality of suffering has broader implications for American society. The church becomes complicit in promoting a distorted historical memory that erases and marginalizes the voices of those who endured the historical trauma in the first place.

Concepts of lament lay just beyond the biblical literacy of secular American culture. Many people of various faiths are familiar with the Psalms. Recited at weddings, funerals, and political events, the Psalms have a firm place in civic life. William Holliday points to Psalm 23 as a secular icon.[10] This familiarity is not surprising in a country where the Christian faith has enjoyed a high level of civic privilege in its formative centuries. Although lament and anger are strong themes, many of the Psalms designated for liturgical use by American denominations focus instead of thanksgiving and celebration.[11] In effect, such decisions remove the painful experiences from Christian life, erasing the corporate engagement of painful emotions from church communities and leaving its members ill-equipped to grieve and unify with their neighbors.[12] Rebalancing the two modes of the Psalms, praise and lament, provides a richer faith experience which can also apply to the university classroom. Furthermore, the social usefulness of the Psalms, as Walter Brueggemann argues, employs a full range of perspectives in a faith community.[13] In this way, the Psalms are essential in teaching history, helping to recover diverse and often painful historical perspectives cut from the American narrative in favor of civic celebration.

Pedagogy of Lament

The practice of lament is a tangible embodiment of these best practices for classroom and community engagement. Lament is practiced by considering the points of view of the oppressed, including their anguish, desire for deliverance, and hope for positive outcomes. As presented in the Old Testament books of Lamentations and the Psalms, Biblical concepts of lament offer valuable insight into how this may be accomplished in the classroom. The structure of the Psalms suggests an approach particularly well suited to engaging students of history in the classroom. The works of Soong-Chan Rah, Denise Hopkins, and others, present starting points for understanding the cultural context for institutional programming and classroom pedagogy, respectively.

To view slavery and oppression as injustice in the Biblical sense, situates the suffering of people of African descent with a broader historical narrative that serves to separate it from presuppositions the intended audience may have regarding United States history and "the dominant American cultural ideology of success, continuity, and avoidance of anything messy."[14] Equating American slavery with the broader injustices of the human experience provides a bridge for historical understanding for a social justice-minded audience, bringing a "painful situation to speech" and affirming the reality of the lingering impact many people still experience.[15] A pedagogy of lament patterns teaching this traumatic experience after the structure of corporate Psalms of lament. While many scholars officially reference eight particular Psalms as a communal lament, about a third of the Psalms express individual or collective anger or distress to God concerning the events faced by the historical nation of Israel.[16] Still, the five parts of the official communal laments have pedagogical value for the historian.[17]

The first part of communal lament is the address to God, often expressed in the "how long" phrase that opens many Psalms of lament. Biblically, the temporal reference is rarely an actual question but rather a statement of outrage intended to draw attention to an enduring difficult circumstance, to the point of feeling dead or no longer relevant to the world.[18] Similarly, the fact that chattel slavery remained an integral part of American society for several centuries should spark outrage for the student of history, as it did for those Africans and African Americans under its subjugation. The complaint or petition from the Psalmist to God then continues to express feelings of death and invisibility that historians have debated as the concept of social death.[19] While enslaved people certainly made cultural spaces for themselves within the constructs of slavery, their legal status and often violent physical treatment represented constant threats to their recognized humanity.

After the events at Mother Emanuel, politicians, faith leaders, and academic administrators gave messages of hope about looking forward to the day when hate crimes and racial discriminations are no more. They spoke of the next steps and discussions to help people understand each other. Fewer people desired to reflect on events already passed in sadness. Claus Westermann points to praise and lament as the dual nature of the Psalms as two "basic modes of thought when humans turn to God with words."[20] Likewise, the events at Mother Emanuel made clear the necessity of acknowledging suffering in addition to looking forward to better days. The lament of the Psalms is examined as a biblical structure that validates the human experience, gives words to the oppressed when they are too tired to speak themselves. In the same way, lament is also a biblical response that can be applied to the work of the historian in interpreting violent historical experiences with a pedagogy that extends beyond the collective memory of both instructor and student.

The second part of communal lament is the lament itself and the specific description of the circumstance. How does one ethically represent a life that appears so briefly, in some cases just a name on a chart or a paragraph in a newspaper? As a historian of slavery, my responsibility is to present individual lives as fully as possible, as if I was explaining to their family members what happened to their lost loved ones. And while details are sometimes elusive, we must do our best to figure out the kinds of things that they dealt with from day to day. We owe it to those who have passed to represent their lives fully, regardless of what we think their impact has been. As historians, the desire to weave a narrative is essential to our writing and teaching. But in the case of slavery, the overall story can be mundane. Recovering and incorporating ordinary people into the histories of slavery goes a step beyond analyzing slave systems and their regional variation. Some students have trouble reconciling the suffering doled out by their ancestors, and others would rather listen to stories of the triumph of their distant historical relatives. Lament is a practice largely missing from the American church. In her study *Journey Through the Psalms*, Denise Hopkins notes that the majority of the Psalms omitted from lyrical use in the Lutheran *Book of Worship*, the Episcopalian *Book of Common Prayer*, Catholic *Lectionary for Mass*, and the *Hymnal for the United Church of Christ* are those of lament. Lament constitutes 40% of all Psalms, but only 13% of the hymnal for the Churches of Christ, 19% of the Presbyterian hymnal, and 13% of the Baptist hymnal. Without care, this trend can obscure the interpretation of slavery.[21]

One symptom of a culture prioritizing praise over lament is the impulse to celebrate the minority of enslaved individuals who triumphed over slavery throughout its existence, often at the expense of those who remained. Students love the rebellions, but the very term resistance is an already misbalanced concept within historical inquiry. For several generations of scholars, studying slave resistance meant looking at how enslaved Africans disrupted plantation life and challenged their owners through sabotage, armed rebellions, or merely running away. And while these are undoubtedly appropriate avenues for intellectual exploration, if we are not mindful, this approach can very quickly treat enslaved Africans as mere victims of a growing capitalist economy by privileging the stories of those who beat that system. Such an approach is inadequate without a persistent effort to recover the lives and points of view of the enslaved themselves.

Adherence to this ethical standard is problematic for various reasons, but two stand out—the first stems from modern-day American culture. Quite simply, we favor a good underdog story. Whether it be the American Revolution or one of the Rocky movies, we love to hear about someone overcoming adversity. Unfortunately, this tendency in teaching slavery focuses on active slave resistance, those secret plots, surprise rebellions, and bloody revolts. However, real life is not an action movie, and the desire to discover the cinematic features of our past does not get us any closer to recovering individual lives. The second factor is that a primary focus on escape is that it offers a gendered interpretation of history that privileges the male experience. Males were most likely to engage in active resistance, which did not happen very often. These are the enslaved former African warriors or the ones with fewer attachments on the plantation. Mothers were less likely to rebel and leave their children. The story of those who remained enslaved encompasses a vast majority of the enslaved experience. Though not always exciting, it is the story of our ancestors. The truth of the experience is in the mundane.

The third part of communal lament consists of a national confession of trust that their prayers will be heard. To examine how enslaved African Americans lived and adapted to slaves, wider society, and its varying degrees of personal autonomy is what affirmed enslaved humanity. To lament their experience and not privilege those who escaped is to recover their point of view and contributions. It is to understand the question of "How long, O Lord." Our pedagogy should focus on the longing for *maranatha*, or divine rescue, in which people hoped and endured. This shift is not to deemphasize the celebration of escaping bondage, but to appreciate all parts of the enslaved story equally. Recovering the mundane illuminates the motivations and spirituality of enslaved people who relied on a theological framework of lament throughout a great range of situations that stretched beyond legal definitions of freedom and helps students of history understand the fourth section of communal lament, the specific request for divine intervention in a defined historical circumstance.

Enslaved people understood that freedom from slavery also often implied an end to life. Several Psalms echo the feeling of being dead, separated, or under the earth. The systematic nature of slave-related legislation in the history of the United States guaranteed that free people of color faced significant barriers after release from slavery. A change in legal condition by no means implied an end to oppression. As such, a complete application of the Psalms of lament embraces the full range of human emotions, from anger to hopelessness. Aware of a legal system stacked against them, enslaved people hoped for far more than freedom but rather a full range of hopes and dreams that spanned family and vocational operations. Considering these desires serves to represent the lives of the enslaved beyond simple regard for exterior legal status and instead as human participants in the legacy of the United States. Examining the varied individual iterations for divine intervention with the language of the Psalms informs a historical pedagogy that reaffirms the humanity of Africans and African Americans in America in a way that resonates with students. Additionally, it allows comparison with other marginalized groups like European immigrants in the nineteenth and twentieth centuries, engaging discussion from historical students from various backgrounds

The final stage of communal lament is a vow of praise. Praise for delivery from slavery offers several opportunities for embracing the complete narrative of Psalms of lament. Recent events, such as the institution of Juneteenth as a national holiday in the United States, demonstrate that the multitude of experiences of African Americans throughout slavery was not monolithic. Different people celebrated the end of slavery in various ways and at different times. Juneteenth commemorates the day African Americans in Texas learned of the Emancipation Proclamation from federal troops over two years after its signing. The ensuing celebration certainly fulfills the Psalms vow of praise when a specific petition is addressed. Still, the delayed nature at the heart of Juneteenth combined with racial discrimination that continued from another century through practices like convict leasing and Jim Crow laws are a reminder of why lament should be an ongoing theme in historical teaching of an evolving story. Desegregating schools did not grant equal access to education. The Voting Rights Act did not end voter intimidation. Barack Obama's election as president did not end racism.

Hopes for Lament

Higher education institutions possess an opportunity and responsibility in the ideological conversations confronting the trauma of racism and slavery. When the general validity of college education is under scrutiny, engagement with this topic is a necessity. Where the university has struggled in the past to remain publicly relevant, proper curricular intervention and extra-curricular programming, potentially amplified due to high profile race-based incidents, can reach hitherto uninterested audiences. But how should that story be told?

Engagement with the violence that undergirds American society has not been the strong suit of the Ivory Tower.

Faith-based collegiate institutions, who often gesture toward social justice in their broader missions, have a unique opportunity to address these issues in many facets of university life, all the way down to pedagogy. Responsible engagement with experiences many deem traumatic is paramount to the academic work that undergirds community healing. Because the darker moments in history are often less familiar in American celebration culture, like the enslaved experience on Charleston plantations, such ideas are often controversial. Confronting lesser-known narratives is a best practice for ethical teaching as it has a secondary effect of greater inclusion of historical voices.

Such classroom interventions are not new, of course. The idea of culturally responsive teaching goes back for over two decades. Conceived as a pedagogical method to improve diverse audiences' learning outcomes, it combines prior experiences with standard cultural references among the students.[22] Scholars like James Banks articulate a curriculum model that moves instructors toward social justice. In a model that mirrors how liturgical lament has been altered in the twentieth-century church and is now under reconsideration by many, Banks' model includes concepts and contributors previously excluded from the curriculum of similar topics to re-examine their value. Inclusions of historical memory of diverse audiences in the teaching of racial violence, and employing new and unfamiliar voices, force personal problem-solving in conceptualizing social action. The classroom, too, can be a "site of conscience."

The oft quoted historic saying that repeats itself is exhausting for the practicing historian. Instead, history is far more elusive, altering its cycles just enough to fool those not paying close attention while frustrating others of us convinced we experience the same events repeatedly. Nevertheless, the study of our shared history, or at least how we remember it, can offer a path forward for those with a willingness to learn. History makes clear that the work of racial reconciliation is similar to that of a Psalmist, a process of self-reflection and lament. Recognition of the task ahead is not a cause for despair but rather another call to muster in the constant quest for justice, inclusivity, and democracy.

BIBLIOGRAPHY

Billman, Kathleen D. and Daniel L. Migliore. *Rachel's Cry: Prayer of Lament and Rebirth of Hope*. Cleveland: United Church Press, 2006.

Brown, Vincent. "Social Death and Political Life in the Study of Slavery." *American Historical Review* 114, no. 5 (December 2009): 1231–49.

Brueggemann, Walter. "Hurt to Joy, From Death to Life." *Interpretation* 28, no. 1 (1974): 3–19.

Brueggemann, Walter. *The Message of the Psalms*. Minneapolis: Augsburg, 1984.

Coogan, Michael D. *A Brief Introduction to the Old Testament*. New York: Oxford, 2009.

Gay, Geneva. *Culturally Responsive Teaching: Theory, Research, and Practice*. New York: Teachers College Press, 2000.

Holladay, William. *The Psalms Through Three Thousand Years: Prayerbook of a Cloud of Witnesses*. Minneapolis: Fortress Press, 2000.

Hopkins, Denise Dombkowski. *Journey Through the Psalms*. St. Louis: Chalice Press, 2006.

Meyer, Lester. "A Lack of Laments in the Church's Use of the Psalter." *Lutheran Quarterly* 7, no. 2 (Spring 1993): 67–78.

Rah, Soong-Chan. *Prophetic Lament: A Call for Justice in Troubled Times*. Downers Grove, IL: InterVarsity Press, 2018.

Rules of The Department of Education. Chapter 0520-XX-XX, Prohibited Concepts in Instruction. Tenn. Code Ann. § 49-6–1019, 2021.

Westermann, Claus. *Praise and Lament in the Psalms*. Atlanta: John Knox Press, 1981.

NOTES

1. Gillian Brockell, "Plantation Reviews: Some white people don't want to learn about slavery at plantations built by slaves," *Washington Post*, August 8, 2019.

2. Adam Parker, "Under scrutiny, historic Lowcountry plantations consider their role in dialogue on race," *The Post and Courier*, July 4, 2020.

3. Dylan Roof shot and killed nine people at Emanuel AME Church in Charleston, South Carolina on June 17, 2015.

4. International Coalition of Sites of Conscience website; www.sitesofconscience.org.

5. This leglislation is part of a set of laws to address Bullying and Harassment. Rules of The Department of Education, Chapter 0520-XX-XX, Prohibited Concepts in Instruction (Tenn. Code Ann. § 49-6-1019, 2021).

6. Denise Dombkowski Hopkins, *Journey Through the Psalms* (St. Louis: Chalice Press, 2006), 5. Kathleen D. Billman and Daniel L. Migliore, *Rachel's Cry: Prayer of Lament and Rebirth of Hope* (Cleveland: United Church Press, 2006), 14.

7. Soong-Chan Rah, *Prophetic Lament: A Call for Justice in Troubled Times* (Downers Grove, IL: InterVarsity Press, 2018), 24.

8. Rah, *Prophetic Lament*, 21, 22.

9. Rah, *Prophetic Lament*, 22.

10. William Holladay, *The Psalms Through Three Thousand Years: Prayerbook of a Cloud of Witnesses* (Minneapolis: Fortress Press, 2000), 359–71.

11. Hopkins, *Journey Through the Psalms*, 5.

12. Walter Brueggemann, "Hurt to Joy, From Death to Life," *Interpretation* 28, no. 1 (1974): 3–19.

13. Walter Brueggemann, *The Message of the Psalms* (Minneapolis: Augsburg, 1984), 19.

14. Hopkins, *Journey Through the Psalms*, 79.

15. Hopkins, *Journey Through the Psalms*, 30.

16. Hopkins, *Journey Through the Psalms*, 80.

17. Michael D. Coogan, *A Brief Introduction to the Old Testament* (New York: Oxford, 2009), 370.

18. Hopkins, *Journey Through the Psalms*, 83, 85.

19. This concept references the decades long debate over the formation of various diasporic black cultures within the confines of the middle passage and American slavery. Such individuals were alive and sentient, but treated as if they were without social value. The conversation centered on how new cultures developed and adapted to the exigencies of slavery and in the absence of legal and cultural recognition by the dominant social class. Vincent Brown, "Social Death and Political Life in the Study of Slavery," *American Historical Review* 114, no. 5 (December 2009): 1231–49. Brown argued that African culture formation can arise in response to, rather than only in resistance of, the slave system. Therefore, the establishment of African-American culture was not always in resistance to the social order that slave owners desired, but rather a movement by and for African Americans on their own terms, completely removed from materialistic notions of property the dominant class.

20. Claus Westermann, *Praise and Lament in the Psalms* (Atlanta: John Knox Press, 1981), 122.

21. Hopkins, 5. See also Lester Meyer, "A Lack of Laments in the Church's Use of the Psalter," *Lutheran Quarterly* 7, no. 2 (Spring 1993): 67–78.

22. Geneva Gay, *Culturally Responsive Teaching: Theory, Research, and Practice* (New York: Teachers College Press, 2000).

Chapter Seven

Teaching History in Mississippi

Lament as Pedagogy in an Era of Suffering, 2008–2022

Otis W. Pickett

The great Mississippi writer William Faulkner is often credited with the phrase "To understand the world you first have to understand a place like Mississippi." After having lived in MS for fourteen years, teaching Mississippi's people from K-12 to college students (at both public and private universities), to incarcerated learners to adults in the broader public, I am beginning to understand what he meant by that statement. The things we have been grieving and lamenting as a nation from 2016–2020 have been manifold, including, but not limited to, racist, misogynistic and xenophobic language from a sitting President, a global pandemic, the death of George Floyd, the ongoing effects of systemic racism driven by white supremacy, the capital insurrection and attempts of the President to delegitimize a national election (just to name a few). These things have caused many of us to reflect on history and pedagogy in unique ways. Of course, I am still helping my students process and make sense of the past, but how does that help them maneuver a modern landscape where the past is all around us and the legacy of the past is directly informing the present? I have found, over the last four years, that my students are more openly political, are either more hardened toward resisting justice work or more active in pursuing justice, and are exhausted, anxious, fearful, and unsure of the future. How do we as historians, professors and scholars meet them in this space, called the classroom, where we are walking them through history, but also coming alongside them in a particularly stressful moment in our nation's history with tools for mental and spiritual flourishing?

Some might argue that it is not the role of the professor to address or speak to these experiences of our students, that helping our students navigate the present is not our job and that I might be promoting activism or presentism. That perspective says that we are simply here as conduits of presenting completely "objective" information and making sure our students are prepared via memorization of "the material": dates, facts, events, people and how they happened in chronological order. However, this is not the way I was taught. My professors saw me as a human being with struggles; they talked me through several situations and related to me not just as a professor, but as a person. Further, I cannot disassociate from my context and therefore, recognizing how much more our students are being shaped by our cultural moment, there is a great need in the modern classroom to walk with our students and help them with the tools to process what they see unfolding daily in American life. As professors and teachers we are doing more than delivering content. We are helping students to shape how they see the world and their place in it. We are providing students with tools and frameworks to think about the world and we model daily how we, as scholars, think through and deal with the pain, injustice and brokenness so common on our modern landscape.

What is comforting about teaching in Mississippi is that this has all happened here before and, as the writer of Ecclesiastes says "there is nothing new under the sun." It would be accurate to say that Mississippians are well practiced in painful experiences over the long durée of American history and have become accustomed to grief, sorrow and lament as a coping mechanism for survival. Mississippians, and more specifically Black Mississippians, have survived oppressive slavery, Jim crow segregation, racial violence, decades of murder via lynching (the highest percentage of lynching of any state in the nation) and simply killing or removing anyone who would resist the status quo. More generally, Mississippi has survived gripping poverty, pandemics, a lack of labor opportunity, underfunded educational systems of oppression, floods and hurricanes, mass incarceration, disfranchisement and lack of adequate healthcare, which are present issues that historians should not weigh in on as activists. Living in Mississippi, the question for me has not been "should we engage in these issues" but "how can we not" engage and act to dismantle these oppressive structures? In some ways, there is not a group of people better equipped to lead the nation in lament and processing grief than the people of the state of Mississippi. In this chapter, there are several examples, occurring in a classroom community, where lament became a part of the pedagogical practice, but was also a response to student distress. The students and I were brought together into a shared practice of lament simply because there was nothing else we could do. It became a way that we processed what was happening in our community, it served as a vehicle to connect the past with the present, and ultimately helped all of us develop an empathetic perspective as we were living through very difficult times. It also allowed us time to stop, grieve and really sit in the brokenness. It was only out of that brokenness and through sharing in that pain that we could understand and try to do something to make a difference.

Teaching in Mississippi for almost fifteen years, I often found that in many of the spaces where I was lecturing or teaching, it could be very healing for the audience to affirm their frustrations and to spend a few minutes processing together what had happened. Connecting my talk to the lived experiences of the audience and spending some time grieving a situation before moving on to the next point is often appreciated. Mississippians very much appreciate not being talked "to" but talked "with." A growing number of students in our classrooms feel this way. There is something about teaching that requires us to do more than "stand and deliver" a lecture. Indeed, as Faulkner reminded us "the past is not dead. It's not even past." To be sure, many of the themes, ideas, experiences and events that happened throughout history are currently ongoing in Mississippi as well as the nation at large. While Mississippi is the place where applying time for lament became professional practice for me, it did not begin here.

It was September 11, 2001 and I was entering my junior year as a history major at Clemson University. That day we watched in horror as massive airline jets flew into the World Trade Center and the Pentagon. My roommate and I did not possess the words or frameworks for the grief, the shock, the fear and the sense of uncertainty we all possessed. We called loved ones and tried to get some sleep that night. The next morning, we headed to our Second Half U.S. History course taught by Dr. Richard Saunders. Dr. Saunders had spent the previous day in deep study and thought. He came to class that morning, but instead of covering he topic at hand, he started class with something else. I remember he said (I am paraphrasing) "in order to better comprehend what happened yesterday you have to understand the context of Afghanistan over the last forty years and the relationship that the United States has with this region." He then proceeded to help us understand the conflict with Afghanistan and the Soviets, the role the U.S. played in the rise of the Taliban and the world in which Osama Bin Laden worked and moved throughout the nineteen eighties and nineties. This helped me make sense of what happened; it was comforting and it gave me tools to understand. What he was doing was more than instructing, he was caring for and ministering to his students. As a Christian, I sat back and marveled. This professor, at a public university, understood grief, lament and time needed to collectively process better than most Christians at Christian Universities. How much more should Christian professors be setting aside class time to help our students process, grieve and lament what is going on around them?

In the Fall of 2003, I began studying for an M.A. in Theological Studies at Covenant Seminary. One of the first African-American professors hired at Covenant, Dr. Anthony Bradley, was teaching a course in systematic theology that Fall and I was very eager to take his class. One day in class Anthony decided to read through a website and the accompanying message boards of supposedly "fellow Christians" who shared in the theological tradition of the seminary and also possessed a pro-Confederate perspective. I remember Bradley saying "I just wanted y'all to be aware about what some of those in our camp are writing and saying about me being the first African-American to be a Professor at Covenant Seminary." On the website there was an article that the seminary published on Bradley's hiring. Bradley proceeded to read each of the comments below the article and stopped multiple times as the comments contained some of the most racist, offensive and hateful language that I and the other seventy plus students in the course had ever heard. In 2004, several of us in the course "wept over the sin and hate contained in this website. We lamented over the pain this must have caused Bradley, who should have been celebrating being a newly minted Ph.D. and receiving that first coveted teaching job. Instead, he found himself being attacked by Christians in his own theological tradition who were posting hateful language about him simply because of his race."[1] Bradley led us through a practice of recognizing what happened, giving us and himself space to process what had been written and to grieve and lament what was done, and then he moved on to teach one of the most amazing classes I have experienced, walking us through one of the Psalms of Lament. We grieved and corporately lamented. We prayed for Dr. Bradley and for the people who posted the comments. It was something I would never forget. My understanding is that, since these incidents, many of the people who were responsible for this website have called Dr. Bradley or reached out to repent and apologize.

In the Summer of 2006, I accepted a graduate assistantship at the Avery Center for African American History and Culture in Charleston, SC. This center is not only a marvelous resource for archival research at the College of Charleston, but it possesses a tremendous collection of primary sources and materials through museum collections that tell the stories of the African-American experience from enslavement through the Jim Crow era and up to the modern Civil Rights movement. Part of my job was to give public tours of the center, and many of these tour groups were comprised of African Americans from all over the country. Historians estimate that a large percentage of African Americans in the United States can trace some sort of familial connection back to Charleston as one of the largest ports of entry for enslaved Africans in the eighteenth century up to 1808. For the visitors to Avery, the history is not just history. It is familial. It is felt. It continues to be both a source of pride, but also of pain as similar structures of a white supremacist system are still in place in America today.

As the tour progressed from the exhibit on the institution of slavery up through the Jim Crow era, I found it necessary to stop at times and let our visitors voice their own frustrations and put words to their grief. In other words, we needed to just stop and process what we just saw. In contrast to many of the historical spaces in Charleston from 2006–2008, the Avery center told the whole story about slavery. This was the first time many visitors to the city saw slavery and segregation as a central component of Charleston's history. There was often great emotion, pain, anger and frustration that other spaces in the city did not include this history, as well as great concerns visitors had about why it was not included. As a staff docent and someone who grew up in Charleston, I not only shared the history, but also helped folks to process how this happened, and why other spaces didn't want to display this history. We often stopped and had dialogue and many times we wept and experienced grief together over not only the historical suffering, but the ongoing cover-up of that suffering. Serving at the Avery Center taught me many valuable lessons, but one of them was that human beings are more than just receptors for information and knowledge; we are complex individuals with experiences and emotions and those need to be considered when teaching material that is difficult.

In 2008, Ph.D. studies and teaching brought me to Mississippi. Many come to Mississippi and they often come to observe and critique. They go back home with stories mostly beginning with "you'll never believe what I saw." Mississippians know this and so they pride themselves on hospitality. However, few who visit want to live there or be a part of moving Mississippi forward in any long-term capacity. Most people just want to come for a short time, observe, complain and have a story or an experience they can take back home or to write about. It's almost like Mississippi has become America's scapegoat, a place and a people sent off into the wilderness carrying the sins of the nation with it. Few see value in the state or acknowledge the incredibly robust literary and music history of the state or consider the hundreds of Civil Rights activists still working and living around the state who helped shape this country, men like John Perkins, James Meredith, Medgar Evers or women like Fannie Lou Hamer, Ida B. Wells and Myrlie Evers-Williams. These are Mississippians who profoundly changed the landscape of our nation, and their spirit lives on through hundreds of initiatives, organizations, activists and in classrooms across the state. Indeed, as the songwriter JJ Grey says "good things are going on. . . . there in Mississippi." I truly love Mississippi and am honored to have lived there.

However, Mississippians have other memories too. Mississippi sees itself as the true "deep South" and a kind of guardian of white Southern culture.

There isn't much looking outside the border and even less of an interest or concern in what folks outside of those borders think of Mississippi. As the historian Jim Silver once said, "Mississippi is a closed society." Therefore, you might be asking the question: what was it like teaching Mississippi history, the history of slavery, the Civil War, Reconstruction and Redemption in Mississippi in these "troubling times": Sometimes I feel as if I am less a historian and more of journalist, counselor, reconciler, pastor, and therapist simultaneously telling my students "we have been here before. This is continuity over time. We will get through this," and asking the question "in light of what we have talked about today and also what you have seen in history, what will our own responses look like?" Living in Mississippi, in many ways, is like living in the past as if one has been transported back and knows what's to come. Every historian I have worked with or known in Mississippi feels this weight. We teach the past, but the past isn't really past in Mississippi. It's the present. There are echoes of the past all around us and it is incumbent upon the historian in Mississippi to help their students navigate their modern landscape as well as the state's history.

For instance, I believe we are living in our own kind of third "redemption era" in Mississippi (and perhaps the nation at large) where crime and punishment against African Americans is at record highs and a Lost Cause driven memory has reached a fever pitch. Mississippi politicians have also emboldened the current electorate with the current political moment. For instance, a candidate for the U.S. Senate named Chris McDaniel, using the Mississippi State Flag (the last flag in the country to bear the Beauregard Confederate Battle Flag) in his campaign signs and paraphernalia, recently displayed a sort of otherworldly combination of these two realities on the MSNBC show "Morning Joe" filmed live in Oxford, MS on September 14, 2018. The interviewer "asked McDaniel how he would speak to Mississippi's 38 percent of African-Americans and how he would convince them you are not a danger to them." McDaniel responded: "I am going to ask them, after 100 years, after 100 years of relying on big government to save you, where are you today? After 100 years of begging for federal government scraps, where are you today?"[2]

It is interesting that McDaniel puts this mark at 100 years as 100 years ago was also the high point of lynching in Mississippi, the activist work of Ida B. Wells, the incarceration of African Americans at Parchman Penitentiary, and the use of the Confederate Flag in the newly developed state flag that would fly as a symbol of racial oppression. As the nineteenth century gave way to the twentieth, there was a re-immersion of the KKK across Mississippi, disenfranchisement as a result of the Second "Mississippi Plan," codified in the Constitution of 1890, which said that Mississippi's constitution using poll taxes, literacy clauses and grandfather clauses was absolutely constitutional.

Either McDaniel is ignorant of the historical record or he simply didn't care. While Mississippi has made great strides, particularly in removing the Confederate imagery from the state flag in 2021, it is still fraught with violence and oppression toward people who are considered non-white or non-native (another way of saying that they were not born and raised in Mississippi) and rhetoric like McDaniel's only continues that long century of oppression for people of color in Mississippi.

How are we teaching in this context? I have attempted to focus my attention on classroom pedagogy and provide some examples of how lament can be used as a teaching tool both with traditional classroom students at The University of Mississippi, Mississippi College and with non-traditional higher education college courses at Parchman Penitentiary as well Central Mississippi Correctional Facility, which offered college courses through the aforementioned institutions via the Prison to College Pipeline Program.[3]

Mississippi has the highest poverty rate in the nation and simultaneously the lowest percentage of citizens that own a passport. I have taught many college students who have rarely or never been outside the state. There is also a kind of detached pride that Mississippians have in isolation. Many are proud of their state's experience and how different it is from other states; some distrust outside perspectives and use kinship networks to bring in those who are acceptable and keep out those who would critique or challenge the status quo. Many children who grow up poor in Mississippi and cannot leave to experience other spaces simply accept this system. Others in the middle hope to benefit from it one day and are hesitant to challenge it.

This means that in Mississippi change comes slow. Silver mentioned that "In Mississippi this slowly accelerating historic change is seen not as a legitimate outcome of classic American values but as a criminal conspiracy against sanctified institutions."[4] Writing in the early 60's, Silver found deep parallels between the 1850s and the 1950s,

> which remind us that Mississippi has been on the defensive against inexorable change for more than a century, and that by the time of the Civil War it had developed a closed society with an orthodoxy accepted by nearly everybody in the state. The all-pervading doctrine, then and now, has been white supremacy, whether achieved through slavery or segregation, rationalized by a professed belief in states' rights and bolstered by religious fundamentalism. In such a society a never-ceasing propagation of the 'true faith' must go on relentlessly, with a constantly reiterated demand for loyalty to the united front, requiring non-conformists and dissenters from the code be silenced or, in a crisis, driven from the community. Violence and the threat of violence have confirmed and enforced the image of unanimity.[5]

This is something I have grown accustomed to, having lived in Mississippi for almost two decades. My great uncle married a Mississippian and raised his family in Jackson. I have invested in Oxford, Clinton and Jackson for the last fifteen years. My youngest daughter was born pre-mature and spent almost two years in the NICU and later in the PICU and is buried in Mississippi. I have spoken, taught and labored across the state on a number of issues from K-12 public education, to mass incarceration to advocating for changing the state flag.[6] However, I will never be a Mississippian. I will always be an outsider. As a history professor and educator, I have grown comfortable with this role of bringing an outside perspective. Yet also as someone who deeply loves and cares for Mississippi, I can't help but think that Mississippi can be better. I see the remarkable work happening in communities across the state, in the ministries of people like John Perkins, Jemar Tisby and James Meredith. In the work of people like Patrick Weems, Susan Glisson, Stuart Rockoff, Chokwe Lumumba, Jesmyn Ward and W. Ralph Eubanks. There are so many amazing people doing amazing things in Mississippi. I think to myself what could be if people just listened to them.

My introduction to using lament as pedagogy came when I was teaching as a graduate instructor at the University of Mississippi in 2008. That same year, the Chancellor at the University of Mississippi, Dr. Dan Jones, decided to ask the University of Mississippi Band to stop playing the song "From Dixie with Love," which contained a trigger at the end of the song for the student body to chant "the South will rise again." My friend Ben Guest was working on a documentary at the time called "The South Will Rise Again."[7] Ben was able to get footage of the Mississippi Chapter of the Ku Klux Klan, who decided to come to campus and protest this decision by the Chancellor. While teaching my students about the Lost Cause, Redemption and the rise of the KKK in the early twentieth century, my students' intellectual learning environment was also a place where the KKK was currently active. One day during class we stopped to just acknowledge this, process and it and figure out what we could do as a class in response to the KKK's presence. Artair Rogers, the African-American student body president at the time, along with interns from the William Winter Institute were organizing a "Turn Your Back on Hate" rally where they decided to march into a space on campus next to where the KKK were protesting and to read, in unison, the university's mission statement.[8]

At a public university, we took time to stop, recognize what was happening, corporately grieve the incident, lament the continuity of ongoing racism, process the history behind the organizations and agree as a class towards something we could all do to be a part of change. These actions are a part of the process of grief, lament and response to injustice. These became common practices in my classrooms from 2008–2013 at the University of Mississippi and they, I believe, formed more thoughtful and empathetic students who were able to see, in their surroundings, deep connections and continuity to what they were studying in the classroom. In 2013, my higher education career would take me to Mississippi College, which is a member institution of the Coalition of Christian Colleges and Universities (CCCU). Here, it was expected that I connect what we were learning in the classroom to the student's faith journey. I did not realize it at the time but the next nine years would include the deaths of multiple Americans of color, the rise of the Black Lives Matter movement, the election of Donald Trump and the vitriolic, racist, misogynistic and xenophobic language that came with his election and presidency, a Covid-19 pandemic, and the death of George Floyd, which sparked protests around the country including in Mississippi, both in Jackson and in Clinton (the home of Mississippi College).

There were multiple occasions across the nine years I taught at Mississippi College when we engaged in the practice of lament in the classroom. One time a student's church in Alabama had been burned to the ground and we stopped to pray for the members, the families and for her specifically. Other times, the ongoing unnecessary deaths of Black Americans would cause us to stop, acknowledge what happened, help our students process the history and context of racialized violence and try and figure out ways that we could best love and care for our African-American neighbors on campus through diversity and inclusion initiatives such as CURE.[9]

One example of using the practices of grief and lament occurred in the context of Parchman Prison via the Prison to College Pipeline Program. My colleague Dr. Patrick Alexander (Associate Professor of English and African American Studies at the University of Mississippi) and I were teaching an interdisciplinary course entitled "Justice Everywhere: The Lives and Writings of Ida B. Wells, Fannie Lou Hamer and Barack Obama," during the summer of 2015. Just a few weeks into the course a massacre of nine African-American Christians happened at Mother Emanuel AME church at the hands of a racist and Lost Cause adherent. Growing up in Charleston and knowing many of the families affected made it very difficult to teach during this time. Half of my time I was spending preparing for the next class and the other half was spent weeping and grieving with relatives, friends and my former pastor in Charleston, a man named Rev. Herman Robinson. As I walked into class that day, I knew the students were struggling and I was struggling. Instead of covering the topic at hand that day, I spent the time helping the students understand the context of racial violence in Charleston from the early seventeenth century up through the Civil Rights movement and beyond. A colleague of Dr. Alexander's named Dr. Ann Fisher-Worth, who is widely regarded as one of the best poets in the state of Mississippi, was in attendance as a visitor that day. She wrote the following poem:

> "Take that flag down,"
> Says the old inmate whose name
> I don't know, who sits across from me
> In the circle in the Parchman
> Prison classroom where I've come
> with Patrick and Otis, my colleagues
> who teach the history of civil rights,
> where they talk and I listen
> about Fannie Lou Hamer, about
> the Mississippi Freedom
> Democratic Party and *I'm sick*
> *and tired of being sick and tired,*
> and where Otis, who's white and comes
> from Charleston, struggles not to weep
> as he talks about the last few days
> In Charleston. *Take that flag down,*
> the old man repeats, *still wont nothing*
> *change. Flag ain't nothing but a bandaid.*
> Ann Fisher-Wirth[10]

We spent time letting the students also share about the violence they had experienced in Mississippi and of stories they had heard from friends and relatives about racial violence in the past. We corporately shared, we grieved, and we ended up writing essays on the impact of racial violence in places like South Carolina and Mississippi and the affect it can have particularly on populations of people of color. Later during that class, "one of the most meaningful share sessions happened after we had screened a film that had focused on Parchman's connection to civil rights activism during the 1960s. We had joined students in watching and discussing the 2010 PBS documentary Spies of Mississippi, which focused on the Mississippi Sovereignty Commission and its role in monitoring civil rights activism and incarcerating African Americans involved in the civil rights struggle—African Americans like Clyde Kennard, whom the Commission framed. Kennard was sentenced to seven years at Parchman and died soon after his release."[11] We learned that when "Kennard's case appears in the film, emphasis is placed on the fact that Kennard—a U.S. army veteran who had previously taken classes at the University of Chicago—wanted to attend the University of Southern Mississippi (USM), and knew that doing so would integrate that institution. The film reveals that Kennard's decision to apply to USM was considered a threat to the status quo of white supremacy in Mississippi. While Kennard's application was pending, ten dollars' worth of 'stolen' chicken feed was conveniently found on the Kennard family farm. The film makes clear that the state—with the help of the Sovereignty Commission—planted it there."[12]

It was clear that after "PTCPP students watched this segment of the film in the summer 2015, a collective moan came up from them that we can only describe as palpable frustration. During the share session that day, and in the remaining share sessions during the rest of the term, our students began to express how the often unspoken challenges surrounding their lived experiences at Parchman were being corroborated—at least in part—by their collective witnessing of and responding to Kennard's story, and through our group discussions of African American literature and Civil Rights history. The students began to make ever more personal connections between what they read, saw, and heard about the Jim Crow racial caste system and its vestiges in the contemporary criminal justice system. Through their often painful employment of personal anecdotes, PTCPP students articulated historical continuity: they conceptualized anew the long history of civil rights struggle in the United States as they drew striking parallels between the harsh realities of their everyday lives at Parchman and the system of racial injustice confronted by the civil rights heroes and heroines they had been studying all summer. In sum, by creating opportunities for PTCPP students to decipher and discuss such historical continuity within Parchman's gates—and thereby cultivating among our students a sense of self-recognition in a site premised on human disappearance—we had taken a decisive step toward affirming their humanity and honoring their college-credit-earning goals at one and the same time."[13]

Another incident came in 2016, when I wrote a plea to Mississippians to change the state flag, which was the last state flag in America to contain the Confederate Battle Flag in its canton. The response, at the time, was incredibly mixed. I received emails of support and emails encouraging me to leave Mississippi. I am certain my colleagues and my university were drawing the ire of several Mississippians who thought I was being too much of an activist.

That semester I taught an interdisciplinary course on race and the south with a colleague in English Literature. Part of the class was walking students through the choice I made to write this plea and to help them process what symbols meant in terms of what they communicate about a society's values and how the memory of the Civil War was still being invoked to promote racial oppression in Mississippi. Many times, my students stopped to pray for me, to encourage me and to grieve that many of their fellow citizens and some of their family members were decrying my name and pushing for me to leave Mississippi College and Mississippi. Many of those students today have become colleagues. One teaches now in the Psychology Department at Mississippi College; one is working on justice issues as an attorney in Alabama and one became an instructor in the Prison to College Pipeline Program at Central Mississippi Correctional Facility. I was able to watch my students practice lament, see them grieve and observe them come alongside their professor in love and care. The many semesters of practicing lament in my classrooms were modeling to students that what we are reading, studying and doing in these classroom spaces were deeply connected to their lives.

Finally, as the death of George Floyd came amid a national pandemic, I found that the practice of lament became a daily part of my lesson plans and teaching. Daily, we found ourselves grieving and lamenting lost loved ones, national suffering, ongoing injustice and living under the rule of a President who seemed to care very little for the plight of the poor, oppressed and marginalized people of the United States. The pandemic was also hitting the African-American population in Mississippi very hard. Taking daily time in class for lament, prayer and the reading of scripture ministered to my students during an incredibly stressful time for them. At the end of the 2020–2021 school year, many commented in my teaching evaluations and to me privately how important that time was to them. I had chosen to set aside a few minutes during each class to check on my student's mental health, ask what was burdening them, pray for their burdens and remind them that I was here for them if they needed me. It might seem as if this was "wasted class time" to those historians that feel that every minute should be filled with content, but I found the opposite to be true. My students were more focused and determined to understand the material because their minds and spirits were in a better place to receive and to share. Because we had taken the time as a learning community to practice mental health (and I am making the argument that spending time in grief and lament is good for mental health) then the remaining time of class was incredibly fruitful. Those semesters were the greatest teaching semesters I have experienced in my fifteen-year teaching career—in the middle of a pandemic. The times caused us all to stop, to recognize what was happening around us and to pray.

Lament was a constant theme of those prayers and there are many places in the bible that offered examples of times when God's people lamented over the course of five thousand years. We learned from history that we were not alone in suffering. We learned that grieving and lament helped us survive.

BIBLIOGRAPHY

Fisher-Wirth, Ann and Maude Schuyler Clay. *Mississippi*. San Antonio: Wings Press, 2018.

"Mississippi Won't Send A Democrat To DC: Chris McDaniel," Morning Joe, MSNBC. https://www.msnbc.com/morning-joe/watch/mississippi-won-t-send-a-dem-to-dc-says-chris-mcdaniel-1320405571532.

Pickett, Otis W. "Race and the American Church, Part III." https://www.reformation21.org/articles/race-and-the-american-church-part-iii-1.php.

Pickett, Otis and Patrick Alexander. "The Prison-to-College Pipeline Program: An Ethical, Education-Based Response to Mass Incarceration in Mississippi." *Journal of African American History* 103, no. 4 (Fall, 2018): 702–16.

Silver, Jim. *Mississippi: The Closed Society*. Jackson, MS: University Press of Mississippi, 2012.

"The South Will Rise Again." https://vimeo.com/11076828.

NOTES

1. Otis W. Pickett, "Race and the American Church, Part III," https://www.reformation21.org/articles/race-and-the-american-church-part-iii-1.php. It should also be noted that one of the chief architects of the website has contacted Bradley, repented and sought forgiveness.

2. "Mississippi Won't Send A Democrat To DC: Chris McDaniel," Morning Joe, MSNBC, https://www.msnbc.com/morning-joe/watch/mississippi-won-t-send-a-dem-to-dc-says-chris-mcdaniel-1320405571532.

3. https://ptcpp.olemiss.edu

4. Jim Silver, *Mississippi: The Closed Society* (Jackson, MS: University Press of Mississippi, 2012), 3.

5. Silver, *Mississippi*, 3.

6. Otis Pickett, "Let Confederate emblem on Mississippi flag go," *Clarion Ledger*, April 7, 2016, https://www.clarionledger.com/story/life/faith/2016/04/07/my-faith-let-confederate-emblem-mississippi-flag-go/82722980/.

7. "The South Will Rise Again," https://vimeo.com/11076828.

8. https://catalog.olemiss.edu/2008/fall/university/mission.

9. www.mc.edu/equity.

10. Ann Fisher-Wirth and Maude Schuyler Clay, *Mississippi* (San Antonio: Wings Press, 2018).

11. Otis Pickett and Patrick Alexander, "The Prison-to-College Pipeline Program: An Ethical, Education-Based Response to Mass Incarceration in Mississippi," *Journal of African American History* 103, no. 4 (Fall, 2018): 702–16.

12. Pickett and Alexander, "The Prison-to-College Pipeline Program."

13. Pickett and Alexander, "The Prison-to-College Pipeline Program."

Chapter Eight

A Pedagogy of Healing

Karen Johnson

What is history for?

In his powerful 1963 essay, "The Fire Next Time," James Baldwin argues that "To accept one's past—one's history—is not the same thing as drowning in it; it is learning how to use it."[1] As a historian, I am wary of anyone who wants to "use" the past. If not done carefully, using the past can objectify the dead by using their stories for our own purposes, rather than first understanding them on their own terms. This would not honor the humanity of our predecessors. Furthermore, when people look for a usable past, they often want to find something that will further current agendas.[2]

Baldwin was not talking about simplifying the past for present purposes, however. Instead, he imagined a study of the past that brought transformation to those in the present, which is what we want our students to experience in our classrooms. Baldwin was calling the "innocents," white Americans who did not know their racial past or how their actions affected the lives of black Americans, to begin to see. Baldwin hoped that by learning their history and acknowledging their current complicity in racial oppression, white Americans would break free from the shackles of "innocence" and work for a new day. Baldwin was right about the potential for the innocents to change. I have experienced some of that change in my own educational journey.

How can we teach for transformation in our history classrooms, not in ways that caricature the past for current agenda, but in ways that allow for authentic transformation as we study America's complex racial history? Creating a classroom characterized by lament can further this goal. I write as a practicing Christian seeking not just to help students *think* better but to help them *be* more of who they were made to be.[3]

Lament, however, cannot simply be added to a history class where the goal is to transfer content from the teacher to the student. Instead, the teacher must intend to craft a class where love is the beginning and the telos. This type of teaching fosters connections between the student, the teacher, and the subject; it spins a web of connection and love between all the actors in the classroom.[4] This essay, in fact, is a product of the web of love I tried to weave with my students at Wheaton College, an evangelical Christian institution, and our subjects in a class on race, justice, and reconciliation in US history. As we lamented, we thought about our practice metacognitively. I wrote and they responded, pushing my arguments further, making new connections, and raising important questions.

The web of connection teachers spin with their students also extends to the dead in the type of history class I am describing. This position reflects a reality fundamental to Christian faith: that the communion of saints includes both the living and the dead.[5] One ought not think of knowledge as something inert and objective that is "out there." Rather, knowledge is embodied in people who lived, people made in God's image who are worthy conversation partners. This knowledge, and the truths within it, require the living to listen and respond. Because love is an action, not a feeling, the students and the teacher must respond to the truths they encounter with action. As the master teacher Parker Palmer argues, obedience means to "listen with a discerning ear and respond faithfully to the personal implications of what one has heard."[6] If our goal is love, lament can help teachers and students weave the web of love as we study America's racial past. Because love requires action, it helps us reach forward to future generations. As the historian Margaret Bendroth argued, "we are connected to people of the world today, and to those who created the world with their own labor. We are also connected with other invisible people: the unknown generations yet to be born."[7]

What is lament?

Most simply, lament is talking to God about suffering. Suffering's foundation, Christians would argue, is first original sin, and then both the continued sin of people and the systemic sin we inhabit. Most western conceptions of sin do not account for its fullness; they tend to operate on an individual level. Lamentations is consistent with other parts of Scripture when it speaks of both personal sin and corporate sin. It also testifies to the suffering of those who sin and those who are its victims.[8] More profoundly, lament is a gift because it offers its practitioners a way to walk in the midst of suffering, naming their pain as they turn to God, asking God to act, and choosing to trust that God will fulfill God's promises. The Psalms and the book of Lamentations in the Hebrew scriptures offer a liturgy of lament that teachers can bring into their classrooms explicitly through individual and corporate prayer. More fundamentally, lament can help students and teachers build a set of habits or dispositions that characterize how they approach their subjects, students, God, creation, and themselves.

Lament begins with turning to God with a complaint. This turning to God is a crucial first step. Especially for those like me, white evangelicals raised with a theology of praise that only infrequently laments, it can be easy to turn away from God when we encounter suffering.[9] Too often, people's theology is not thick enough to account for suffering.

After turning to God, we lay out our complaints. For instance, in Psalm 13, David asked "How long, Lord? Will you forget me forever? How long will you hide your face from me? How long must I wrestle with my thoughts and day after day have sorrow in my heart? How long will my enemy triumph over me?"[10] In the book of Lamentations, the prophet Jeremiah described in exquisite detail the destruction of Jerusalem in 586 B.C. In a genre known as a funeral dirge, Jeremiah opened with the cry "How deserted lies the city, once so full of people! How like a widow is she, who once was great among the nations! She who was a queen among the provinces has now become a slave."[11] Jeremiah's funeral dirge is not like other contemporary dirges.[12] It offers no hope, mourning the irrevocable nature of what has happened.

But there is hope in the book of Lamentations, eventually. Lament's great hope is that even amid asking *why* suffering has happened and how long it will continue, we remember *who* we are talking to.[13] The one we talk to is sovereign and could have stopped the suffering. In Lamentations, Jeremiah said that Jerusalem's sin caused the suffering, "Jerusalem has sinned greatly and so has become unclean," but also recognized that God brought the suffering, as the city says, "Is there any suffering like my suffering that was inflicted on me, that the Lord brought on me in the day of his fierce anger?"[14]

Those lamenting look to this sovereign God as their hope, reminding God of God's character. David's prayer in Psalm 13 referenced God's promise that David was the anointed one, saying, "look on me and answer, Lord my God. Give light to my eyes, or I will sleep in death, and my enemy will say, 'I have overcome him,' and my foes will rejoice when I fall."[15] Jeremiah also hoped in God, praying to God according to God's character: "Look, O Lord, and consider: Whom have you ever treated like this? Should women eat their offspring, the children they have cared for? Should priest and prophet be killed in the sanctuary of God?"[16] Jeremiah also reminded people that "because of the Lord's great love we are not consumed, for his compassions never fail. They are new every morning; great is your faithfulness."[17]

Those lamenting are characterized by three other postures. First, they listen to the voices of the marginalized. Throughout Lamentations, for instance, Jeremiah speaks about the suffering of the vulnerable, especially children and women who are experiencing deep pain because of others' sins. Second, they humbly identify with those who have sinned in lamenting corporate sin and suffering. Jeremiah does not observe that "those other people" sinned. Rather, he says "my sins have been bound into a yoke; by his hands they were woven together. They have come upon my neck and the Lord has sapped my strength. He has handed me over to those I cannot withstand."[18] Third, they choose to trust that God is faithful and good, and will act according to God's character.[19] As Jeremiah wrote, "I say to myself, 'The Lord is my portion; therefore I will wait for him.'"[20] As David cried out, "But I trust in your unfailing love; my heart rejoices in your salvation. I will sing the Lord's praise for he has been good to me."[21]

Lamenting in the history classroom, then, requires teachers and students to see and name the pain of race in American history. This history is heavy, especially for those who bear the scars in the present. We approach the pain and the sin in humility, spinning the web of connection between the living and the dead, including those we abhor. We also should use the opportunity to see others' evil as a chance to look inward, considering the evil in our own hearts. But lament reminds us that we do not enter these relationships with the dead alone; we do not encounter evil and suffering alone. Rather, at the center of the suffering, amid dark clouds, we find God, characterized by *hesed*, or loving kindness. We can cry out to God with their pain and in our pain. We can pray Scripture to God, asking God to fulfill promises to bring justice, to free the oppressed, and to unite those who are different together as one. In these prayers, we can find healing. Then, marked both by the pain and by the healing, we can join God's work of letting the Kingdom come on earth as it is in heaven.

Lament and Historical Thinking

At first glance, history education as love and characterized by lament does not seem to align with most historians' training. In graduate school professors become content experts and refine their ability to think historically. History is not a normative discipline, so historians refrain from telling others what to do. Instead, historians try to uncover what happened in the past, weighing ephemeral evidence and narrating the best true stories about what happened as we are able, understanding what happened in the past from as many perspectives as possible.[22] We recognize that, as the former American Historical Association president Carl Becker observed, "by no possibility can the historian present in its entirety an actual event, even the simplest."[23] Nonetheless, we must strive to observe the distance between the present and the past without collapsing that difference. Refusing to see the difference reduces the past to a faded version of the present. By contrast, historical empathy, arguably the hardest historical thinking skill to teach, demands the historian understand her subjects in their context and temporarily set aside their own ideas of right and wrong. Empathy is not a feeling; it is a discipline. Empathy prevents us from becoming presentist, judging the past by our present standards.

Lament, by contrast, sometimes requires naming actions as evil. If a historian does not do history, temporarily setting aside their own perspectives, before lamenting, lament can collapse into presentism. For instance, imagine a student reading that prior to the Emancipation Proclamation, Abraham Lincoln supported having African Americans leave the United States, moving to Africa or Central America. Say that this student immediately labels Lincoln's position as evil (and probably racist) because Lincoln, like most white people of his time, did not think white people and African Americans could live together. The student will miss the complexity of Lincoln's support for emancipation and the political calculations he made as he tried to make emancipation appealing to white conservatives.[24] The student will also miss seeing how whiteness changed, and how even white abolitionists could support racial hierarchies. The aspect of lament that names the wrong can hinder historical thinking if the historian makes a judgment too quickly without fully considering the context. As one of my students observed, "if a value judgment is made too soon, one can begin to create an emotional connection" with that judgment, limiting the historian's ability to understand what happened.[25]

How, then, can a historian teach her students to lament and do history well?

Humility, which characterizes both lament and historical thinking, can help. To study the past well, we must become aware of our biases and the limits to our knowledge. We must specify our ignorance. Studying history requires setting aside our assumptions about what is right and wrong, forgetting ourselves in a sense, to understand someone else. Humility is also necessary for a historical consciousness, another goal of history education, because historical consciousness allows us to recognize that the norms of our own time and place were historically constructed. In realizing that our "normal" has a history, we can realize our ways of being are neither inevitable nor necessarily ideal.

When lamenting others' sin, the humility of Jeremiah the prophet *and* the humility required for historical study can reinforce one another and lead to new questions as we seek to be obedient to what we encounter. For instance, when my students learn about the immediate abolitionism of Jonathan Blanchard, Wheaton College's first president, they are delighted. Blanchard's commitment to abolition is inspiring. But when they reflect on the land where our college sits, they become more sober. A substantial portion of Wheaton College's land was donated to the school by Warren Wheaton in 1859, the year Jonathan Blanchard became president. Wheaton's generous donation helped the struggling school survive and was made possible in part by Wheaton's grit and determination as a settler in a new land.

But the donation was also made possible by the United States government's recent policy of Indian removal, exemplified in the 1833 Treaty of Chicago. There, the Potawatomie ceded their land to the US government after observing the US expel their neighbors the Sauk from the region in the Black Hawk War a year earlier.[26] While Blanchard grieved the treatment of some Indians, he agreed with their removal and supported their "civilization," a position most Native Americans today see as cultural genocide. Humility in lament and historical thinking would require my students and me not to distance ourselves from this history, but, in obedience, to confess that we are learning on Potawatomie ground, taken both with good intention and deep greed.

In addition to developing a sense of humility, lament can help us strengthen historical thinking by emphasizing human complexity. While a person's actions shape their desires and thus who they are, distinguishing between the person and the action can enable lament and further historical analysis. My students reminded me that recognizing "a certain action as evil [does not] involve bringing judgement to the person who committed the act."[27] Only God, they insisted, brings judgment.

The Black civil rights activist Fannie Lou Hamer can help clarify the difference between naming an action as evil and condemning a person in judgment. Fannie Lou Hamer grew up as a sharecropper in Mississippi. She learned she had a right to vote as an adult when Bob Moses and the Student Non-Violent Coordinating Committee came to Mississippi to register people to vote. When Hamer attempted to register, convinced that Jesus had called her to this action, white policemen arrested her and took her to jail. There, they had black men beat her brutally. Somehow, Hamer forgave their actions. She knew that while the policemen's evil actions were wrong, they were still people God loved. As the historical theologian Charles Marsh argues, Hamer's theology of a welcoming table meant that if her oppressors repented, she would welcome them into her lives. She knew they were not the sum of their actions, and so did not condemn them as humans.[28]

Table Fellowship

Even if a historian is humble and recognizes complexity, when she laments, she names an action as evil, which means judging the past by contemporary standards.[29] What I have offered above can allow lament and historical thinking to coexist, but a tension remains. As we understand it in the twenty-first century, good historical thinking requires setting aside contemporary ideas about right and wrong for a time. Historians have a responsibility to understand as much as we can about the past, to tell as true a tale as possible, and we do not want our current ideas to cloud our judgment. If we use disciplinary standards that reach toward "objectivity," lament cannot be practiced in the history classroom.

But if we practice our craft using the metaphor of the history classroom as "table fellowship," we can foster transformation in our lives and the lives of our students. In table fellowship, we listen to and talk with those around a table about things that matter, not always agreeing. In history, as in any conversation, people need to listen to one another, ask clarifying questions, and do as much as they can to understand another's point of view. Because the dead are at our mercy, historians need to be especially careful to understand and articulate the dead's perspectives faithfully. All the tools of historical thinking are essential for this task, and we must not let ourselves or our students shirk this responsibility.

Table fellowship also requires speaking. It would not be a conversation if one person just listened to the other. The historians—the teachers and the students—must also talk back to the dead. This talking back to the dead must come after wrestling with what we learn. As the scholar Alan Jacobs argues, "any *genuine* kinship with our ancestors must be earned through hard mental work."[30]

Since lament is a form of talking back to the dead, it cannot be the first move in the history classroom. As historians, we have a responsibility to do the work of listening to and grappling with the dead. Historical humility reminds us that we have limited knowledge of the dead. Theological humility reminds us that we see through the glass darkly and, even if we could know all the necessary information about the dead to answer our questions, our sin would corrupt our knowledge. But we also know truth; by common grace all have truth within them. And truth, furthermore, is beyond us and not entirely subject to history. We have a responsibility, therefore, to bring these truths—the truths we encounter in the past and the truths we know in the present—together in lament.

Teaching our students to speak back to the dead can help them progress beyond immature epistemologies. Scholars who study historical epistemologies argue that students, if taught well, will progress in their epistemologies as they become better historical thinkers.[31] Most students are first naïve realists who are looking for the "right" answers about what happened and who want one "true" narrative of the past. This position is understandable and most textbooks, because of how their authors write them, reinforce this epistemological stance. As students grow in their historical thinking skills, many will become naïve relativists, assuming that if historical accounts vary, all are equal, and one story is as good as another. These students do not know how to discern the strength of a claim nor how to use evidence. Mature historical thinkers, however, are critical pragmatists. They realize that historical accounts will, by nature, vary because people ask different questions, use different sources, and interpret sources differently. Importantly, critical pragmatists recognize that not all accounts are equal. They use historical thinking tools to weigh the strength of different historical accounts.[32] Talking back to the dead in addition to teaching students to think historically can help prevent students from remaining naïve relativists, and often by extension, moral relativists who conclude that those in the past had "their truth," which was right for them, but we have our truth, which is right for us.

Let me ground this discussion of epistemology in an example from my US history survey class. As we study Reconstruction and my students read the Ku Klux Klan's 1868 statement of principles that notes "this is an institution of Chivalry, Humanity, Mercy, and Patriotism" intended to "protect the weak, innocent, and the defenseless, from the indignities, wrongs, and outrages of the lawless, the violent, and the brutal; to relieve the injured and oppressed," my students' first thought is to dismiss the statement as self-delusional.[33] I ask my students to think about the context for the KKK, and to ponder how this statement could make sense to those who supported the Klan. But if we left the conversation with an understanding that "the Klan had their truth and I have mine," we would be missing an opportunity. Instead, students must talk back to the Klan and name the evil it embodied—following the example of the Klan's contemporary African American opponents, even as they account for complexity.

While history as table fellowship and lament require grappling with the contextual nature of truth claims, these frameworks can push students to practice critical pragmatism. Students can consider both how their own perspectives are changed by what they have learned and the ways they resist what they have learned. They can think through what criteria to use as they determine what is good. The historian weighs accounts, including their own accounts of good and evil. We do not need to set ourselves completely aside as we reflect on what we have learned about the past. While we must first listen well to the dead to understand them, we should also listen with both the possibility of being transformed and with the possibility that we will disagree with their conclusions.

Shalom: Restoring Right Relationships

Lament and history as table fellowship, then, can help students to be better historians if the teacher helps them resist presentism, and instead struggles with them to understand as best as possible the dead in their contexts. But lament and historical thinking can also help restore Shalom, the way things ought to be. Sin fractured humans' relationships with God, others, creation and themselves. Lament can help heal each relationship.

A Pedagogy of Healing

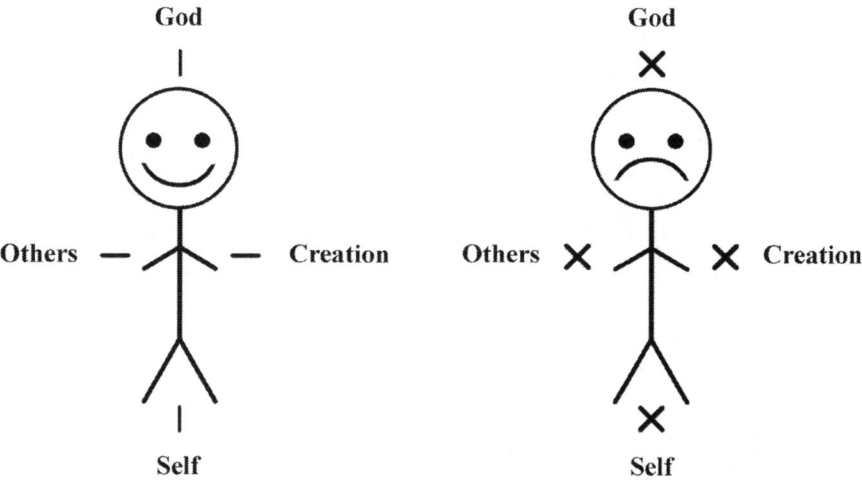

Figure 8.1. Sin's fracturing influence on relationships with God, others, creation, and ourselves

First, lament can reconcile us to God by bringing individual and corporate pain into the truest story: that God is restoring all things. The darkness of individual and systemic sin is heavy. Too often, from our perspective, God's people cried out and God was silent or did not deliver them. But death is not the final word. As one of my students observed, "both teachers and learners can guide one another to look to God as they reckon with the true stories of the past. [We do this] by remembering that Grand Narrative that God is writing throughout all of history, the story of redemption and reconciliation."[34] Teachers and students must bring the true stories of hurt and pain into this Grant Narrative. As the priest and teacher Henri Nouwen argued, "All of ministry rests on the conviction that nothing, absolutely nothing, in our lives is outside the realm of God's judgment and mercy."[35] Nouwen called pastors to be living memories of God, revealing "the connections between our small sufferings and the great story of God's suffering in Jesus Christ, between our little life and the great life of God in us."[36] Similarly, teachers and students can connect the pain they encounter in the past to the pain and suffering of Jesus.

Second, lament can help restore people's relationships with one another. It can be hard for Christian students to learn about the sin in the church's past for many reasons. Students of color may question the truth churches claim to represent. White students may resist narratives portraying heroes of the faith as racist. Remembering the complex stories that reveal how the church and Christians were complicit in racism is hard and uncomfortable, and one response is to try to distance oneself from those other Christians, imagining oneself to be better, somehow. This distancing, however, contradicts the humility central to lament and history. Seeing the sin in the past can, instead, drive us in the present to examine ourselves, searching for sin.

Forgiveness can also help build a connection when we encounter appalling things. In a 1962 sermon, Martin Luther King, Jr. said, "we must recognize that the evil deed of the enemy-neighbor, the thing that hurts, never quite expresses all that he is. An element of goodness may be found even in our worst enemy."[37] Forgiveness, according to King, "does not mean ignoring what has been done or putting a false label on an evil act. It means, rather, that the evil act no longer remains as a barrier to the relationship."[38] Forgiveness is not what the German theologian and activist Dietrich Bonhoeffer called "cheap grace," given to those who do not repent.[39] It is obedience to Jesus, who told his disciples to forgive those who sinned against them seventy times seven times. Even as we forgive, we weep over people's intransigence as Jesus did over Jerusalem because truth had been hidden from the people's eyes and they would suffer because of their sin.[40]

As my students and I thought together about how historical thinking and lament can form us as people, several described how these practices, applied as we studied the past, could bring about right perspectives of themselves, the third relationship to be restored. Both lament and history require humility about ourselves and awe toward God. As Sam Wineburg, one of the leading scholars of historical thinking, argues, "of the subjects in the secular curriculum, [history] is the best at teaching those virtues once reserved for theology—humility in the face of our limited ability to know, and awe in the face of the expanse of human history."[41] Repeatedly, my students emphasized how humility helped them think rightly of themselves. One student observed that historical empathy and lament helps us "remember the complexity within ourselves."[42] Another suggested that "lamenting injustice done to yourself, people like you, or your ancestors brings self compassion. It is important to acknowledge the hardship and the fact that it took strength to continue through it and overcome it."[43]

Part of restoring a right relationship with oneself is acting, which is consonant with lament and learning. As the professor of evangelism Soong-Chan Rah observes, lament ultimately requires action. True education, Palmer argued, leads the learners to some form of action in obedience. Talking to God about suffering can help us find our voices, can show us that in listening to the voices of the dead and of God we can be transformed, can reveal that we can shape our spheres of influence, small as they are. One student observed that our hope in God is "not a passive hope. We remember the past and the pain that the church has caused and look with hope towards the future and ultimate healing of all things while at the same time living into that hope in the present. We should be healing and reconciling agents now, living in faithfulness of our future eschatological hope in the world to come."[44] Or as another put it, "it is important not just to 'sit' with the knowledge we learn, but also see ways we can help our communities grow and reckon with our racial pasts."[45]

Last, lament can help heal humanity's relationship with creation. While there are several ways to consider consequences in this realm, I emphasize place in my teaching. Paying attention to place requires acknowledging our embodied nature as human beings. As people living in particular places, we can seek their good or, perhaps through neglect, contribute to their commodification or destruction. My classes that study America's racial past explore Wheaton College's racial history, digging into its abolitionist founding, subsequent exclusion of African American students, and continuing racial dynamics.[46] One student's observation resonated with many: "when I found out about Wheaton's participation in racism, I felt angry and deeply saddened. I felt angry because no one had ever told me about this . . . I felt deeply saddened because I realized sin can be found everywhere and has caused so much destruction."[47]

Seeing how sin shaped their immediate context made my students think about how they could work for good in the places they inhabit. One student observed "I can often feel self righteous and denounce places that have seen a lot of sin occur in them as 'bad.' By judging them, I fail to see how God is redeeming them . . . If I really think there are sinful features of a place, isn't it more productive for me to actively and humbly follow Jesus in the work he is already doing instead of standing on the sidelines pointing fingers?"[48] Studying and lamenting the history of their beloved school also helped my students see the ordinariness of seeking a place's good in everyday life. One observed that studying local history countered the feeling of being overwhelmed by the whole of America's racial past: "by studying Wheaton's racial past I am able to ground myself and contribute toward God's plan for restoration here in my community. Through lament, I am able to understand that I am not the hero of this story, and through grounding myself in a specific place, I am able to effectively join in the reconciliation effort in a meaningful way."[49] Justice, this student said, "while it can come in large movements, also occurs in daily life," in the places where we live. Knowing one's local history can help one to love the place rightly. One student reflected that "Only when I see [this school] rightly do I feel that I can love it truly, as Jesus calls me to do."[50] The opposite of love is not hate but apathy. We love when we see the faults of a place or a person and choose to remain in relationship. In doing so, we hold fast in connection to those places and people outside ourselves.

Conclusion

"While the life of the mind is critical in historical study," one of my students wrote, "the historical enterprise can also shape [the] life of the heart and soul that can connect with others and with God."[51] I would add that historical study combined with lament can also help students and teachers connect with their places, thus contributing to the restoration of all things.

When James Baldwin called for the "innocents" to begin to see, he observed that "to accept one's past—one's history—is not the same thing as drowning in it; it is learning how to use it."[52] Knowledge does not necessarily lead to righteousness and justice.[53] Instead, we—the teachers and the students—must become the sort of people who create knowledge in love and then use it for love, joining God's work in restoring right relationships to God, to ourselves, to others, and to our places, both in the past, in the present, and for future generations. How do we use this past well? We listen and, in love, let the past transform us.

In this way, our classrooms can become places that are not somehow removed from "real life," up in the "ivory tower." Instead, they can become places of healing, restoration toward wholeness, and reconstituting the broken relationships that characterize our lives. We can also come to see that our habits in the classroom *are* real life. My students reminded one another that "the postures we adopt while in the classroom will carry us for the rest of our lives, as we are lifelong learners," and that since "anywhere can be a classroom . . . we can continue to learn and make those connections."[54] Cultivating the habits of lament and historical thinking will help us stop the habit of "neglect[ing] stories that complicate our narrative."[55]

Practicing lament as a liturgy in the history classroom can give us all a holy freedom to do these works of service. At any point, God could make all things right. In lament, we ask why God does not, even as we trust in God's character and receive power to join God's good work.

BIBLIOGRAPHY

Arnold, John H. *History: A Very Short Introduction*, 1st ed. Oxford: New York: Oxford University Press, 2000.

Bain, Ken. *What the Best College Teachers Do*. Cambridge, MA: Harvard University Press, 2004.

Baldwin, James. *The Fire Next Time*. New York: Random House, 1992 (1962).

Becker, Carl L. "What Are Historical Facts?" *The Western Political Quarterly* 8, no. 3 (September 1955): 327–40.

Bendroth, Margaret. *The Spiritual Practice of Remembering*. Grand Rapids, MI: W.B. Eerdmans, 2014.

Bonhoeffer, Dietrich. *The Cost of Discipleship*. New York: Pocket Books, 1995.

Jacobs, Alan. *Breaking Bread with the Dead: A Reader's Guide to a More Tranquil Mind*. New York: Penguin Press, 2020.

Johnson, Karen J. "Shaping Affections: Remembering Our Racial Pasts and Institutional Lament." *Christian Scholar's Review* 67, no. 4 (2018): 445–54.

Lee, Peter and Denis Shemilt. "A Scaffold, Not a Cage: Progression and Progression Models in History." *Teaching History*, no. 113 (2003): 13–23.

Maggioni, Liliana. Bruce VanSledright, and Patricia A. Alexander. "Walking on the Borders: A Measure of Epistemic Cognition in History." *Journal of Experimental Education* 77, no. 3 (Spring 2009): 187–214.

Keating, Ann Durkin. *Rising Up from Indian Country: The Battle of Fort Dearborn and the Birth of Chicago*. Chicago: University of Chicago Press, 2012.

Marsh, Charles. *God's Long Summer: Stories of Faith and Civil Rights*. Princeton, New Jersey: Princeton University Press, 1997.

McKenzie, Robert Tracy. *The First Thanksgiving: What the Real Story Tells Us about Loving God and Learning from History*. Downers Grove, IL: IVP Academic, 2013.

Palmer, Parker J. *To Know as We Are Known: A Spirituality of Education*, 2nd ed. San Francisco: Harper & Row, 1993.

Rah, Soong-Chan. *Prophetic Lament: A Call for Justice in Troubled Times*. Downers Grove, IL: InterVarsity Press, 2015.

Rah, Soong-Chan. *The Next Evangelicalism: Freeing the Church from Western Cultural Captivity*. Downers Grove, IL: IVP Books, 2009.

Satia, Priya and Malcolm Foley. "Responses to 'Is History History?'" September 7, 2022. https://www.historians.org/publications-and-directories/perspectives-on-history/october-2022/responses-to-is-history-history.

Shi, David E. and Holly Mayer, eds. "Organization and Principles of the Ku Klux Klan (1868)," in *For the Record: A Documentary History of America*, 5th ed., vol. 2. New York: W. W. Norton, 2013.

Smith, David I. "Christian Mind □≠□ Christian Pedagogy." *International Journal of Christianity & Education* 21, no. 1 (March 1, 2017): 2–5.

Sweet, James. "Is History History? Identity Politics and Teleologies of the Present." August 17, 2022. https://www.historians.org/publications-and-directories/perspectives-on-history/september-2022/is-history-history-identity-politics-and-teleologies-of-the-present.

VanSledright, Bruce. *The Challenge of Rethinking History Education: On Practices, Theory and Policy*. New York: Routledge, 2011.

Vorenberg, Michael. "Abraham Lincoln and the Politics of Black Colonization." *Journal of the Abraham Lincoln Association* 14, no. 2 (Summer 1993): 22–45.

Vroegop, Mark. *Dark Clouds, Deep Mercy: Discovering the Grace of Lament*. Wheaton: Crossway, 2019.

West, Cornell. *The Radical King*. Boston: Beacon Press, 2016.

Wineburg, Sam. *Historical Thinking and Other Unnatural Acts: Charting the Future of Teaching the Past*. Philadelphia: Temple University Press, 2001.

NOTES

1. James Baldwin, *The Fire Next Time* (New York: Random House, 1992), 81.
2. Robert Tracy McKenzie, *The First Thanksgiving: What the Real Story Tells Us about Loving God and Learning from History* (Downers Grove, IL: IVP Academic, 2013), 15–16.
3. See David I. Smith, "Christian Mind ≠ Christian Pedagogy," *International Journal of Christianity & Education* 21, no. 1 (March 1, 2017): 2–5, https://doi.org/10.1177/2056997116687982.
4. Parker J. Palmer, *To Know as We Are Known: A Spirituality of Education*, 2nd ed. (San Francisco: Harper & Row, 1993).
5. The idea that those of us living are united with the dead strikes many of my Protestant students as odd. They have thought about the cloud of witnesses, but they have not thought about an ontological unity with the dead. This cognitive dissonance results, in part, from the history of Protestantism. As historian Margaret Bendroth argues, "from its earliest days, Christianity was known for the strength of the invisible tie" between the living and the dead until the Reformation began to sever the connection, a disruption that has ebbed and flowed to the present when, "the dead have begun to disappear in earnest." Margaret Bendroth, *The Spiritual Practice of Remembering* (Grand Rapids, MI: W.B. Eerdmans, 2014), 103, 107.
6. Palmer, *To Know as We Are Known*, 89.
7. Bendroth, *The Spiritual Practice of Remembering*, 118–19.
8. Soong-Chan Rah, *Prophetic Lament: A Call for Justice in Troubled Times* (Downers Grove, IL: InterVarsity Press, 2015), 56–57.
9. Soong-Chan Rah, *The Next Evangelicalism: Freeing the Church from Western Cultural Captivity* (Downers Grove, IL: IVP Books, 2009).
10. Psalm 13:1–3, NIV.
11. Lamentations 1:1, NIV.
12. Rah, *Prophetic Lament,* chap. 2.
13. Mark Vroegop, *Dark Clouds, Deep Mercy: Discovering the Grace of Lament* (Wheaton: Crossway, 2019), chap. 1.
14. Lamentations 1:8, 12, NIV.
15. Psalm 13:3–4, NIV.
16. Lamentations 2:20, NIV.
17. Lamentations 3:22–24, NIV.
18. Lamentations 1:13, NIV. See also Rah, *Prophetic Lament*.
19. Vroegop, *Dark Clouds, Deep Mercy*, chap. 4.
20. Lamentations 3:24, NIV.
21. Psalm 13:5–6, NIV.
22. I use the definition of history as "true stories" about the past that John Arnold offers. John H. Arnold, *History: A Very Short Introduction*, 1st ed. (Oxford: New York: Oxford University Press, 2000). For a recent debate over presentism and the claim that history should be objective, not normative, see James Sweet, "Is History History? Identity Politics and Teleologies of the Present," August 17, 2022, https://www.historians.org/publications-and-directories/perspectives-on-history/september

-2022/is-history-history-identity-politics-and-teleologies-of-the-present; Priya Satia and Malcolm Foley, "Responses to 'Is History History?,'" September 7, 2022, https://www.historians.org/publications-and-directories/perspectives-on-history/october-2022/responses-to-is-history-history.

23. Carl L. Becker, "What Are Historical Facts?," *The Western Political Quarterly* 8, no. 3 (September 1955): 334.

24. For Lincoln's position on colonization, see Michael Vorenberg, "Abraham Lincoln and the Politics of Black Colonization," *Journal of the Abraham Lincoln Association* 14, no. 2 (Summer 1993), http://hdl.handle.net/2027/spo.2629860.0014.204. For a discussion of Lincoln, race, and historical thinking see Sam Wineburg, *Historical Thinking and Other Unnatural Acts: Charting the Future of Teaching the Past* (Philadelphia: Temple University Press, 2001), chap. 4.

25. Ian Davidson, response to Lament Prompt 1, November 1, 2020, author's possession.

26. Ann Durkin Keating, *Rising Up from Indian Country: The Battle of Fort Dearborn and the Birth of Chicago* (Chicago: University of Chicago Press, 2012); Karen J. Johnson, "Shaping Affections: Remembering Our Racial Pasts and Institutional Lament," *Christian Scholar's Review* 67, no. 4 (2018): 445–54.

27. Charlene Peng, Response to Lament Prompt 1, November 19, 2020, author's possession.

28. Charles Marsh, *God's Long Summer: Stories of Faith and Civil Rights* (Princeton, New Jersey: Princeton University Press, 1997), chap. 1.

29. The phrase "table fellowship" is from Alan Jacobs, *Breaking Bread with the Dead: A Reader's Guide to a More Tranquil Mind* (New York: Penguin Press, 2020). Jacobs, an English professor, argues that we should read old books intending to create table fellowship with the authors.

30. Jacobs, 77.

31. Bruce VanSledright, *The Challenge of Rethinking History Education: On Practices, Theory and Policy* (New York: Routledge, 2011); Peter Lee and Denis Shemilt, "A Scaffold, Not a Cage: Progression and Progression Models in History," *Teaching History (London)*, no. 113 (2003): 13–23; Liliana Maggioni, Bruce VanSledright, and Patricia A. Alexander, "Walking on the Borders: A Measure of Epistemic Cognition in History," *Journal of Experimental Education* 77, no. 3 (Spring 2009): 187–214, https://doi.org/10.3200/JEXE.77.3.187-214. The discussion that follows is discipline-specific, but it relates to the developmental model of learning more generally in which students move through four broad categories of what they think knowing is. In this framework, the progression is not linear and could be more advanced in different disciplines. "Received knowers" are concerned with getting the right answers and cannot create or evaluate knowledge. "Subjective knowers" believe knowledge is a matter of opinion and use feelings to make judgments. "Procedural knowers" can follow the discipline's rules and criteria for making judgments, but their knowledge does not affect them outside class. Students at the highest level, "commitment" become independent, critical, creative thinkers that consciously try to use the ways of thinking they have learned throughout their lives. Some of these students are "separate knowers" who detach themselves from ideas, while others are "connected

knowers" who "look at the merits of other people's ideas instead of trying to shoot them down." Ken Bain, *What the Best College Teachers Do* (Cambridge, MA: Harvard University Press, 2004), 42–43.

32. VanSledright, *The Challenge of Rethinking History Education*, 66.

33. David E. Shi and Holly Mayer, eds., "Organization and Principles of the Ku Klux Klan (1868)," in *For the Record: A Documentary History of America*, 5th ed., vol. 2 (New York: W. W. Norton, 2013), 9–10.

34. Maggie Akinyele, response to lament discussion 3, November 26, 2020.

35. Nouwen, Henri, *The Living Reminder: Service and Prayer in Memory of Jesus Christ* (New York, NY: HarperCollins, 1977), 26.

36. Nouwen, *The Living Reminder*, 25.

37. Martin Luther King, "Loving Your Enemies," in *The Radical King*, by Cornell West (Boston: Beacon Press, 2016), 55–64.

38. King, 57.

39. Dietrich Bonhoeffer, *The Cost of Discipleship* (New York: Pocket Books, 1995).

40. Luke 19:41–44, NIV.

41. Wineburg, *Historical Thinking and Other Unnatural Acts*, 24.

42. Bella Girthofer, response to lament discussion 4, December 2, 2020.

43. Lydia Heinig, response to lament discussion 3, December 9, 2020, author's possession.

44. Andrew Lauber, response to lament discussion 3, Nov 19, 2020, author's possession.

45. Don Crowder, response to Maddy Whitmer's response to Lament Discussion 2, November 12, 2020, author's possession.

46. Johnson, "Shaping Affections."

47. Ian Davidson, response to Lament Discussion 2, November 10, 2020, author's possession.

48. Mary Kathryn Daigle response to Andrew Lauber's response to lament discussion 2, November 12, 2020, author's possession.

49. Maddy Whitmer response to lament discussion 2, November 9, 2020, author's possession.

50. Mary Kathry Daigle response to Lament Discussion 2, November 12, 2020, author's possession.

51. Mary Kathryn Daigle, response to lament discussion 5, December 11, 2020, author's possession.

52. Baldwin, *The Fire Next Time*, 81.

53. I am indebted to a conversation between Mary Kathryn Daigle and Maddy Whitmer for the ignorance and knowledge framework here. See Lament Discussion Prompt 5, December 9, 2020—December 10, 2020, author's possession.

54. Maddy Whitmer, response to Lament Discussion Prompt 5, December 9, 2020; Charlene Peng, response to Lament Discussion 5, December 10, 2020, author's possession.

55. Don Crowder, response to Lament Discussion Prompt 5, December 10, 2020, author's possession.

Chapter Nine

A Mourning March

Learning Lament in the Classroom of the City

Gregory R. Perry

In late August of 2014, a new fall term was starting and my seminary class on the *Book of Job* was packed with future counselors and pastors. This would be the seventh time I would lead a group of graduate students through this traumatic story of human misery, a story passed across cultures and generations as a vital tool for cultivating wisdom at the extremes of life and death. Though each of these seven readings applied Job's test of extremes with its usual, intended force, the painful cries and shouted questions outside our classroom in the fall of 2014 broke through the door and barged their way into our syllabus.

Just a few miles from our campus in suburban St Louis, only two weeks before the start of classes, Darren Wilson, a Ferguson Police officer, "shot and killed Michael Brown, an unarmed 18-year- old."[1] Only a month earlier, Eric Garner, another unarmed African American male, had been killed in police custody with a choke hold. Brown's death ignited violent protests in Ferguson, drawing people and media from across the United States to St Louis. These traumatic public events and many others, much more personal, vibrated around and through us as we started reading about "this man who was the greatest of all the people of the east" (Job 1:3).

Among other aims, this reading of the *Book of Job* was designed to help both the instructor and students . . .

- recover the practice of lament in order to respond to God with honest questions, doubts and faith in the presence of human pain and suffering.

- dialogue constructively, yet critically, with diverse wisdom traditions about possible interpretations and responses to human pain and suffering.
- develop their capacity to sit with and listen to those who suffer in our communities, and
- respond with wise, compassionate care both as individuals and as a community.

Educators will notice that these intended outcomes engage all three learning domains—cognitive, affective, and psychomotor. As a story that frames what is largely a book of poetry, *Job* was not designed merely to instruct the minds of ancient students of wisdom. Rather, its author intended also to jolt the hearts and bodies of its readers like a cardiac crash cart. The genres or literary forms of the *Book of Job* are offered as learning resources in themselves; its narrative frame and poetic dialogue are part of the curriculum. In one sense, the tests offered within their reading are not atypical. Every human being faces sickness and death. In another sense, however, Job's tests are severe. Not every parent has to face the sudden death of their child, much less the deaths of all their children in one, violent storm "from God" (2:10). The riveting intensity of Job's drama is the polarity of its extremes. Job's uprightness is electrified and illuminated by Job's steep, hard downfall.

With the *Book of Job*, this essay explores several questions, "What is wisdom? Who is wise? How do members of a wise community interpret and respond to human pain and suffering?" But, because this essay is much shorter than the *Book of Job* and this volume is focused on lament, we will limit our exploration to how teaching, learning, and practicing lament cultivates wisdom in individuals and communities. We will proceed in four steps. First, we will define the practice of lament and describe its literary shape in the wisdom literature of ancient Israel. Second, we will trace the role of lament in the development of Job's character and, by contrast, the significance of its absence in the speeches of Job's "miserable comforters" (16:2). Third, we will critically engage both religious and non-religious wisdom traditions about interpretations of and responses to human pain and suffering. Finally, we will evaluate the learning outcomes of our reading of the *Book of Job* in the 2014–2015 academic year both in the classroom on campus and in the classroom of the city.

The Practice of Lament: Its Historical Source, Theological Significance, and Literary Shape

In this volume, many authors offer definitions of lament, so I will be brief: Lament is an honest cry of pain to God in prayer. Lament is artistically developed pain-into-poetry, often sung together in sorrow before God in worship.

Even individual, personal laments are shared with God and God's people in the sanctuary. Lament relates human misery to God's good character and, thus, asks "Why?" and "How long?." Laments are protest songs that exclaim "things aren't the way they're supposed to be!" There is a rupture in the social fabric, wounds that require remedy, wrongs that cry out for reparation. But, in the community of faith and their prayers of lament, these wounds are aggravated by a sense of abandonment. "Lord, where are you?" Lament is a plea, even a demand, for God's attention and presence, a bridge crossing a perceived chasm between the people's pain and the God, who can make them whole again. "Lord, look, come near, and deliver us!"

Lament expresses deep grief from real loss. So, every lament has a site wound and a history. For example, Jeremiah's collection of *Lamentations* is rooted in the horrors of being on the losing side of war—"Judah has gone into exile" (Lam 1:3). Specifically, the Babylonians, under Nebuchadnezzar II, besieged Jerusalem and burned Solomon's Temple in 586 BCE. As Soong-Chan Rah wrote,

> The funeral dirge is a reality check for those who witness suffering and allows mourning that is essential for dealing with death. Rather than denying reality, *Lamentations* portrays suffering and death in gritty detail.[2]

Most importantly, however, laments not only face life and death fully; they address God about it directly. As Walter Bruggemann summarized,

> Israel and Israelites in their hurt have to do with God, and God has to do with them. . . . Israel knows that one need not fake it or be polite in the divine presence, nor need one face the hurts alone. In the dialogue, Israel expects to understand what is happening and even to have it changed.[3]

As we will see below, this first element of lament, addressing God, is a vital aspect of the development of Job's character and the quality of his theology. While "Job's three friends—Eliphaz, Bildad, and Zophar" (Job 2:11) speak only about God, Job grows in wisdom and understanding by speaking, indeed sometimes shouting, to God. As Brueggemann suggested, Job's God-talk or theology is developed "in the dialogue."

Practicing the Poetry of Lament Develops Job's Character in the Story

Students of Israel's wisdom literature seem to have begun their curriculum studying the *Proverbs*. But, according to Ellen Davis, the goal of their education was unique:

> The lure that the Israelite sages offer their students has little or nothing to do with personal professional advancement. Although they speak of "gaining discipline for success," consider how they define success: the establishment of righteousness, justice, and equity.... The Bible shows no interest whatsoever in abstract knowledge—that is, knowledge abstracted from goodness.[4]

In the opening scenes of the *Book of Job*, its author introduces the main character as a master of proverbial wisdom. "This man was blameless and upright; he feared God and shunned evil" (Job 1:1). In the heavenly council, "the LORD" has not only taken notice, he repeats the narrator's glowing description and asks "the Satan" whether or not he has "considered my servant Job" (1:8). "Does Job fear God for no good reason?" (1:9). The Adversary's cynical reply strikes at the character of God's covenant bond with Job, calling into question the "integrity," "love," and "goodness" of both. The clear implication is that Job is on the take. And, God is a cosmic helicopter parent, clearing the way for Job to secure his own reputation and interests. Do God and Job love each other freely or is their relationship merely transactional? "The Satan" boldly claims if God withdraws protection and blessing, Job will "curse you to your face" (1:11). Does God take the Satan's bait or does God know more than God is letting on? Students of wisdom will have to keep reading to find out. But, like Job, they will do more than read; they will suffer tests of extremes. At the extremities of life and death, blessing and curse, who will understand? Who will emerge with wisdom?

After this general introduction to Job's story and Israel's wisdom literature, I share several examples of psalms of lament with the class (i.e. Pss 6, 10, 13, etc.), their elements and movement. Then, I ask them to start writing. Divided into groups, each student shares two prayers of lament with his or her fellows in the first month of the semester. Their first lament responds to God on behalf of others who are suffering. The second is born of personal pain. To reset my students' lament-writing in the context of Job's poetry, we walk through a comparison and contrast between Job's cry of pain in chapter 3 and his full-fledged lament in chapter 10.

The fall of 2014, I asked my students and myself: "Have you ever taken a week of vacation days to visit a friend, not a close family member, while they are grieving the death of a child or going through chemo or radiation treatments?" Job's friends did. Though they will deserve correction for what they say later, what Eliphaz, Bildad, and Zophar do for Job before they speak is praise-worthy: They visit him in his affliction (cf. Job 1:11–13; Jam 1:27). Shattering the seven-day silence, however, Job lets out a primal scream that unsettles both his friends and his readers. Though some commentators label it as such, Job's first poem is not a biblical lament. The proper designation is important. For as we saw above, laments are prayers that address God directly. In chapter 3, Job curses (3:8), but he does not curse God as the Satan had said he would (cf. 1:11; 2:5).

Like many who have experienced severe trauma, Job wishes he had never been born. His poem is God-haunted, referencing God in 3:4 and 3:23, but only in the third person. Job wonders why the light shines on those in misery and longs for a death that will not come (3:20–21). Job's world was disintegrating. Instead of anticipating the blessing of gifts, Job calls for curses on his birthday. Instead of praising the one who crushes the sea-monster, Leviathan, Job calls for someone to rouse him (cf. 3:8; Ps 74:13–14). As Norman Habel noted,

The consistent storyline of a pious patriarch responding submissively to the afflictions of heaven is broken suddenly . . . and not resolved until his final words in 42:2–6.[5]

This break, caused by Job's outcry, raises questions about his earlier responses. According to our narrator, "Job did not sin in what he said" (1:22; 2:10). Still, were reciting proverbs (1:21) and resignation (2:9–10) fitting responses to his experiences? While he didn't cross any lines, should not he have questioned such an enormous loss of life, love, and legacy? Did Job's initial responses display a mature perception of his circumstances and the moral vigor of someone who desires, loves, and pursues what is good, just, and beautiful?[6] Was Job wise enough not only to avoid evil, but also to challenge it? With his pain-filled cry in chapter 3, Job acknowledges his life no longer made sense. Though Job had not yet started lamenting, he had started grieving.

Job's turn back to God in grief takes time and steps. Making a half turn, Job continues the theme of his outcry, wishing that God would put him out of his misery and "cut me off" (6:9). However, he turns again in 7:7–21 to address God directly: "Remember, O God, that my life is but a breath! . . . You will look for me, but I will be no more" (7:7). Job resolves to speak out, to complain, to lament to God (7:11; 10:1). Job wants to make sense of what has happened so he will ask the God he thought he knew. "Remember that you molded me like clay. Will you now turn me to dust again?" (10:9). Job has lots of questions, mainly questions. "You gave me life and showed me loving-kindness" (10:12). But, "Why did you bring me out of the womb? I wish that I had died before any eye saw me" (10:18). Key elements of lament emerge in chapter 10. Job addresses God directly. He brings many complaints. He confesses faith in the God who had given him life and love. But, Job's call to action is odd. Instead of seeking rescue or some form of restoration, Job wants God to leave him alone and let him die (10:20; 14:6). Like those who wrote and prayed Psalms 39 and 88, Job cannot yet step towards God in hope. Job cannot yet promise that he will one day, again, praise God. As Ellen Davis has concluded,

> [This] is a further mark of the Bible's persistent realism. . . . [S]ometimes the only act of faith that is possible—for those who suffer and those who minister to them—is to name our desolation before God and to implicate God in our suffering.[7]

Still, Job keeps talking to God. He keeps asking questions. And, as he does, he moves out of resignation into confrontation and argument with God. Job tells his friends, "Though he slays me, yet will I hope in him. I will surely defend my ways to his face" (13:15; 23:4, 7). This is the paradox of wisdom at the extremities of life and death: instead of cursing God to his face, Job argues his innocence before the God he accuses of injustice; he hopes in the God of whom he is terrified (23:1–7, 13–17). Job argues not only for himself, he also represents others who cry for justice (24:1–25). Job wants to know "how often is the lamp of the wicked put out?" (21:17). "Who declares his way *to his face*, and who repays him for what he has done?" (21:31). As Ellen Davis surmised,

> Job rails against God not as a skeptic, not as a stranger to God's justice, but precisely as a believer. It is the very depth of Job's commitment to God's ethical vision that makes his rage so fierce, and that will finally compel an answer from God.[8]

In the brief space of this essay, focused as it is on lament, we will not rehearse the lengthy attempts by Job's friends to explain his trauma with the tropes of conventional wisdom in order to reaffirm their sense of normalcy and moral order. However, this much must be said. Though Eliphaz, Bildad, and Zophar have a lot to say to Job about God, they never talk to God about Job. Never once do they pray for their friend. The most noticeable difference between Job and his friends is that while Job laments, his friends do not.

Engaging Wisdom, Educating for Shalom

We return now to the question, "what is wisdom?" We began to answer above with reference to the opening description of Job as the epitome of proverbial wisdom: "This man was blameless and upright; he feared God and shunned evil" (cf. Job 1:1, 8; 2:3; 28:28; Prov 1:3, 7). However, we also asked, "Did Job's initial, resigned response to the theft of his cattle, murder of his servants, and, especially, the sudden deaths of his children, display the moral vigor of someone who loves and pursues what is good, just, and beautiful?" Job's story and these questions push us toward a more robust description of wisdom.

Plato spoke of wisdom as "a swarm of virtues," but Aristotle described *prudence* or *practical wisdom* as supreme. Prudence stands at the intersection of the intellectual and moral virtues to enable wise people "to determine what is and how to do the right thing in every situation."[9] Plato and Aristotle identified four virtues: *prudence, justice, fortitude*, and *temperance* as features of wisdom, which is the operating system for a life of integrity. Like the biblical sages, Plato and Aristotle agreed that wisdom is much more than "skills for success in life," though not less. It is about perceiving the world and oneself rightly (*prudence*), relating rightly to and for others (*justice*), remaining steadfast with purpose and direction through life's challenges (*fortitude*), and regulating one's emotions towards a desire for what is good (*temperance*). But, for as much as they revere wisdom, the biblical sages start and finish with *awe* or *wonder*: "the *fear* of the LORD is the beginning of wisdom" (cf. Prov 1:7; Job 28:28).

Wonder pushes beyond our ability to adequately describe what we perceive. We are astonished, perplexed, and bewildered! We stand at the limits of human knowledge and look over the edge. Wonder is about self-transcendence or, better yet, a revelation of otherness that can be both ecstatic and terrifying. Thus, wonder is akin to fear in both senses of the word. As William P. Brown points out,

> [though wonder] may begin with a centrifugal push of fear . . . ultimately wonder attracts rather than repels. In wonder, fascination overcomes fear, desire overcomes dread. . . . and with desire comes a new attentiveness . . . a desire to venture forth, to know more, to know the Other.[10]

"Where can wisdom be found? Where does understanding dwell?" (28:12, 20). Acquiring wisdom not only takes intellectual exertion but also demands physical, social, and spiritual exertion. Wisdom requires both research and revelation. In the fall of 2014, as my students and I pursued our own questions in lament, many of us ventured out to sit with our African American neighbors and listen to their pain-filled cries to God about the deaths of their children. Though many went, some expressed resignation and helplessness. Still, others added their neighbors' questions to their own and joined their neighbors' laments to call for change.

In his essays on teaching and learning, the noted Yale philosopher Nicholas Wolterstorff criticized the socialization, acculturation, and academic discipline models of education, because they fail to address the wounds of society. For Wolterstorff, students of wisdom must pursue two tasks simultaneously: 1) developing human knowledge, attitudes, practices, and systems that produce the material and social goods that sustain life; and, 2) remediating the ignorance, dispositions and dysfunction in ourselves and relationships which undermine that production and threaten human flourishing. In other words, Wolterstorff argues, we must educate for shalom and teach for justice. A longing for justice and peace is the heartbeat of lament.

At the beginning of this chapter, we noted how the desired learning outcomes of this course in the *Book of Job* engaged all three learning domains—the cognitive, affective, and psychomotor. Job's friends, Eliphaz, Bildad and Zophar had the traditions, stereotypical scenarios, and sayings of conventional wisdom ready to access. The problem is that the study of traditions and theories often make students comfortable with the status quo and equips them merely to perpetuate it. To address the wounds of society, however, students of wisdom need face-to-face encounters with those who suffer. Moreover, they need a language with which to interpret their experience. Eliphaz, Bildad, and Zophar visited Job in his suffering, but they did not learn the language of lament. To cultivate empathy and equip students of wisdom with a new framework for action, the Job class, along with the entire seminary community, was invited to pray with their feet.

The opportunity to participate in a mourning march was announced as class ended in the fall. When students returned from Christmas break, we not only gathered with hundreds of others from the community on Martin Luther King Jr.'s birthday to consider his "Letter from a Birmingham Jail," many students also engaged in a nonviolent protest against the use of deadly force by police against unarmed citizens, our fellow image-bearers.

> When the bright, cold morning came, we marched down the Delmar Divide toward the Central West End, stopping twice along the way to amplify the witness of our neighbors' grief. In a rhythm of complaint, confession, and petition, again and again we cried out, "Why?" and "How long, O Lord?" By intentionally disrupting business as usual, we called our neighbors to pay attention to the pain, to stand and pray against the violence, and to love all the streets of St Louis, not just those of their own neighborhood.[11]

The police began calling for us to move out of the intersection, where we had circled. But, having arranged ahead of time with them to stop traffic there, we stood our ground. Brittany, one of the young women marching with us that morning, lifted the bullhorn to ask God, "Why have we lost so many of our young, black men? Trayvon Martin, Eric Garner, Michael Brown, Akai Gurley and Tamir Rice were unarmed. Do you see our tears? Do you hear our cries?" No one moved. But, many cried out, "Hear our prayers!" As the march resumed to conclude at a local church, orange-vested "clergy" led chants, "This is what theology looks like!" And, "this is what community looks like!" Experiencing the bitter cold, the honking horns, the tension with police, and the tears of our neighbors within the interpretive framework of lament stoked a sense of wonder that we were touching a wisdom larger than ourselves, across artificial lines of generations, races, and neighborhoods.

Evaluating Our Learning at the End of Job's Story

Near the end of his words, Job imagines signing a public, legal summons that requires "the Almighty" to write out an indictment that details his wrong-doing or to release him (31:35–40). Job's laments have moved him out of despair into contention with God for justice. But, instead of "cursing God *to his face*," Job wants his day in court to hear God "denounce his conduct *to his face*" (21:31). Can a human being summon God to court? The silence is deafening, until a young hotshot lawyer named Elihu steps forward to speak. From 9:32–35, Job has pled for a mediator, an advocate. He needs character witnesses who will stand with him before God. But, Elihu makes the same mistake as Eliphaz, Bildad, and Zophar. He does not believe that God's ways can be questioned. And, thus, he does not believe in lament.

At the end, God speaks with the only person who has spoken to God in lament. But, the LORD (the personal name of God) does not speak to Job from a lectern, he speaks to him from the middle of a storm (38:1). The LORD does not list any charges, for he has not appeared in response to Job's legal summons. Instead, the LORD takes charge of the search for wisdom by cross-examining Job:

Who is this that darkens my counsel?

Where were you when I laid the earth's foundations?

... Who laid its cornerstone—

while all the sons of God sang for joy?

Who shut up the sea behind doors,

when it burst forth from the womb,

when I made clouds its garment

and wrapped it in thick darkness? (38:2–9)

The LORD's response interweaves bracing questions with wondrous experiences designed to reframe Job's imagination, particularly his deconstructive curse on the day of his birth (chapter 3). The LORD's poetry reconstructs the world that had come apart for Job, but with a much grander cosmic framing. With treks to the depths of the earth and the constellations of space, the divine docent guides Job's imagination back to some of the images he employed in his curse and complaints to reinterpret their meaning from a higher vantagepoint.

The "clouds" that Job wished would "darken" the morning of his birth, the LORD compares to swaddling bands which wrap the chaotic sea (cf. 3:5; 38:8–9). Not only did Job's mother release life-giving water from her womb, but the life-giving (and life-taking) waters of the earth are sired and birthed by God (cf. 3:10–11; 38:8, 29). Though Job's grief-clouded mind called mourners to attend his birthday, the angels sing with joy as each new day dawns (cf. 3:8–9; 38:7). In his curse, Job questioned why the heavenly lights shine on those who experience sorrow to a point that they seek death (3:20–21). So, the LORD asks whether or not the clouds and heavenly lights obey Job's voice (38:32–35)? Do you even know the paths to their dwellings? (38:20). Job is astonished into silence (40:4–5). But, the LORD's lesson on the limits of human wisdom is not complete. The wondrous tour continues on a safari out into the wild.

The LORD draws Job's attention to the lioness, the raven, mountain goats, bears, wild donkeys and oxen, ostriches, hawks, and eagles. Each creature is difficult to manage. But, the LORD watches over and provides for each of them. Moreover, the wild beasts who rank first in strength are Behemoth and Leviathan. The LORD asks Job, "Can you trap him?" (40:24). "Can you put him on a leash like a pet?" (41:5). Job had called for someone to rouse Leviathan as a bad omen on his birthday (3:8), but the LORD reminds Job that "no one on earth is fierce enough to rouse him [and] everything under heaven belongs to me" (41:10), including Behemoth and Leviathan. By divine revelation, Job learns that the world is wilder, more wonderous, and less anthropocentric than he had previously thought. He learns that God does not create for efficiency with tight controls. Rather, God recognizes dignity in all creatures, even those that Job dreads. God creates with exotic exuberance "for no good reason" (cf. Job 1:9), that is to say, out of an overflow of life, grace, and freedom.

> God does not rule with an iron fist, grinding the wicked into the dust and coercing (or bribing) obedience from earthly subjects. Rather, Yahweh governs with an open hand. . . . Job's laments of powerlessness and suffering have transformed into powerful weapons of protest. . . . Indeed, by the time he presents his final defense, and silences his friends, Job has developed a hide as tough as bronze (cf. 40:18; 41:24).[12]

Lament is a powerful practice in the cultivation of wisdom at the extremities of life and death. It provides an expanded framework that acknowledges the limits of human wisdom and the importance of wonder in wisdom's advance. Lament offers those who pray a way to talk to God about the terrors of this world, even a way to scream against them, while simultaneously holding on to the God who grounds the human desire for justice and peace.

As Job's laments were addressed directly to God, so God's speech is addressed directly to Job. Job is no mystic. He meets God and wisdom out in the world. As Francis Anderson wrote, "The highest nobility of every person is to be enrolled by God in the school of wisdom. And the school room is the world."[13] Though he had been thrown to the extremities of disease and death, Job, like anyone who survives severe trauma, is called to bold reinvestment in life, vocation, family and community. Despite his friends' failure in the test of extremities, Job reinvested in them, forgave and prayed for them, because lament had led him to a deeper understanding of the God who creates and loves gratuitously, "for no good reason." How could Job become a father again, knowing that he could not protect his children from all the terrors of this life? How could our African American neighbors, still grieving the sudden death of their children, find the strength to march and invite our class participation in their mourning? In part, at least, because their laments not only share a fierce honesty about the wounds of society, they advance the dialogue, they spread hope, and they express a longing for justice and peace that reconfigures our integrity and reframes our wisdom in relation to wonder.

BIBLIOGRAPHY

Anderson, Francis I. *Job: An Introduction and Commentary*. Vol. 14 of *Tyndale Old Testament Commentaries*, edited by D.J. Wiseman. Downers Grove: Intervarsity Press, 1975.

Brown, William P. *Character in Crisis: A Fresh Approach to the Wisdom Literature of the Old Testament*. Grand Rapids: Eerdmans, 1996.

Brown, William P. *Wisdom's Wonder: Character, Creation, and Crisis in the Bible's Wisdom Literature*. Grand Rapids: Eerdmans, 2014.

Brueggemann, Walter. *The Psalms and the Life of Faith*, ed. Patrick D. Miller. Minneapolis: Fortress, 1995.

Davis, Ellen F. *Getting Involved with God: Rediscovering the Old Testament*. Lanham: Cowley, 2001.

Department of Justice Report Regarding the Criminal Investigation into the Shooting Death of Michael Brown by Ferguson Missouri Police Officer Darren Wilson, March 4, 2015, 4. Accessed July 31, 2022. https://www.justice.gov/sites/default/files/opa/press-releases/attachments/2015/03/04/doj_report_on_shooting_of_michael_brown_1.pdf.

Habel, Norman C. *The Book of Job: A Commentary*. Old Testament Library. Philadelphia: Westminster, 1985.

Perry, Gregory R. *The Drama of Discipleship*. Eugene: Cascade, 2022.
Rah, Soong-Chan. *Prophetic Lament: A Call for Justice in Trouble Times*. Downers Grove: Intervarsity Press, 2015.

NOTES

1. Department of Justice Report Regarding the Criminal Investigation into the Shooting Death of Michael Brown by Ferguson Missouri Police Officer Darren Wilson, March 4, 2015, 4, accessed July 31, 2022, https://www.justice.gov/sites/default/files/opa/press-releases/attachments/2015/03/04/doj_report_on_shooting_of_michael_brown_1.pdf.

2. Soong-Chan Rah, *Prophetic Lament: A Call for Justice in Trouble Times* (Downers Grove: Intervarsity Press, 2015), 46.

3. Walter Brueggemann, *The Psalms and the Life of Faith*, ed. Patrick D. Miller (Minneapolis: Fortress, 1995), 68.

4. Ellen F. Davis, *Getting Involved with God: Rediscovering the Old Testament* (Lanham: Cowley, 2001), 95.

5. Norman C. Habel, *The Book of Job: A Commentary*, Old Testament Library (Philadelphia: Westminster, 1985), 103.

6. See William P. Brown's description of wisdom in *Wisdom's Wonder: Character, Creation, and Crisis in the Bible's Wisdom Literature* (Grand Rapids: Eerdmans, 2014), 9–26.

7. Ellen F. Davis, *Getting Involved with God*, 21–22.

8. Davis, *Getting Involved with God*, 133.

9. Brown, *Wisdom's Wonder*, 14.

10. Brown, *Wisdom's Wonder*, 21, 23.

11. Gregory R. Perry, *The Drama of Discipleship* (Eugene: Cascade, 2022), 52.

12. William P. Brown, *Character in Crisis: A Fresh Approach to the Wisdom Literature of the Old Testament* (Grand Rapids: Eerdmans, 1996), 100, 105.

13. Francis I. Anderson, *Job: An Introduction and Commentary* (Downers Grove: Intervarsity Press, 1975), 269.

Index

Afghanistan, 89
Alexander, Ann Field, 26
Alexander, Patrick, 95
Anglo-Saxon Clubs, 36, 43n80
Arbery, Ahmaud, 55
Avery Research Center for African American History and Culture, 91

Baldwin, James, 13, 22, 101, 112
Becker, Carl, 16, 104
Bendroth, Margaret, 102
The Bible: emancipation narratives of, 6; patterns of lament in, 18
Black church, 26
Blight, David, 16
Bonhoeffer, Dietrich, 110
Bradley, Anthony, 90
Bradley, Mamie Till, 46–49, 55
Brer Rabbit, 4–5
Brown, William P., 123
Brueggemann, Walter, 20, 119

Chaney, Fannie Lee, 51, 52, 54, 55
Chaney, James, 49–52, 54
Cone, James, 20
COVID-19, 95
Cridlin, William Broaddus, 32–33, 37

Davis, Ellen, 119–20

Douglass, Frederick, 13–22; Fourth of July speech, 14–18

Ebony, 68, 69
Emanuel AME Church, 76, 80, 95
Evers, Medgar, 61–70, 91
Evers, Myrlie, 61, 62, 63, 65, 66, 67, 68, 69, 91

Ferguson, MO, 117, 124
Floyd, George, 95, 98

Garvey, Marcus, 29
God's Trombones, 6–7
Goodman, Andrew, 50–52, 54–55

Hamer, Fannie Lou, 106
Harris, Joel Chandler, 5
Herman, Judith, 8
Hopkins, Denise, 80
Hughes, Richard, 16

International Coalition of Sites of Conscience, 76

Jackson, James E., 64
Jackson, Jimmie Lee, 52–54, 55
Jennings, Willie James, 20
Jet, 48, 49, 68

Job, Book of, 117, 118, 210–22, 125–27
John the Conqueror, 5
Johnson, James Weldon, 6–7
Jones, Leroy, 3, 4
Juneteenth, 82
Justice: and lament, 20, 45; 51–52, 53–54, 63, 65–67; of God, 8

Katongole, Emmanuel, 19, 22
King Jr., Martin Luther, 53–54, 63, 100, 124
Ku Klux Klan, 28, 92, 94, 108

Lament, 108–11; communal, 79–82; definition, xi, 45; funerals as a form of, 47–48, 50–52, 53–54, 57n18, 61-62, 64, 65; history and, 18; of mothers, 46, 51–52; pedagogy of, 102,104 105, 107; public expression of, 30, 47
Lamentations, Book of, 18–19, 102, 103, 104, 119
Lee, Cager, 53, 54, 55
Levine, Lawrence, 5
Lincoln, Abraham, 68–69, 105
liturgy, 80, 102
Lynching, 27, 29, 30, 40n18

McCaulley, Esau, 20
McDaniel, Chris, 92
McElya, Micki, 69
McLeod Plantation, 75, 76, 77
memory: as myth, 16, 33, 37; Native Americans' role in American, 35; suffering and, 21
Middleton Place, 76
Mississippi, 87, 91, 96; flag controversy, 92–93, 97; history of, 92; Mississippi College, 95
Mitchell, John, Jr., 26–31, 34, 37

NAACP, 49, 59, 62, 64, 65, 69, 71nn12–13
National Memorial for Peace and Justice, 21

Nouwen, Henry, 109

O'Connor, Kathleen, 20
oral tradition, 5; African social structures and, 9; as psychological release, 7, 8–9; WPA slave narratives and, 8
Palmer, Parker, 102, 110
Parchman Penitentiary, 95
Pearl Street A.M.E. Church (Jackson, MS), 62, 63, 64
Prison to College Pipeline Program, 95, 97
Psalms: communal, 80–82; of Lament, 78–80, 102–3; *See also* communal lament

Raboteau, Albert, 7, 8
Rah, Soong Chan, 20–21, 45, 46, 55, 57n8, 77, 78, 110, 119
reconciliation: role of lament in, 22
Reconstruction, 8, 26
Rice, Chris, 22
Richmond Planet, 27, 29–30, 34
Richmond *Times-Dispatch*, 33, 36
Richmond, Virginia: Richmond Normal and High School, 26; segregation in, 26–27, 28

Sands, Oliver Jackson, 28, 32, 33, 34
Schwerner, Michael, 49–52, 55
Selma to Montgomery March, 54
slavery, 5, 75, 81
Song of the South, 5
South Carolina, 76–80, 90–91
Stevenson, Bryan, 22
suffering: avoiding sacralization of Black, 57n8; identification with the sufferer, 19, 26; of Jesus, connected with African American suffering, 7, 49

teaching, 106–107; in Mississippi, 88–89, 91–93, 97; *See also* Prison to College Pipeline Program

Till, Emmett, 46–49, 54: murder as catalyzing moment in civil rights movement, 48
Till, Mamie. *See* Bradley, Mamie Till
Treaty of Chicago, 106
Trinkle, Elbert Lee, 29, 30, 36
Trouillot, Michel-Rolph, 9
Trump, Donald, 95

violence: against funeral participants, 66; bearing witness to, 7–8, 19–20, 27, 47–48
Virginia Pageant of 1922, 31–36

Washington, Booker T., 28
Wheaton College, 102, 111
Wilkins, Roy, 63, 64, 69
Williams, Kidada, 7
Wineburg, Sam, 110
Wolterstorff, Nicholas, 123

About the Contributors

Dr. Patrick Connelly is Associate Professor of history and Department Chair of History and Political Science at Mississippi College. He is a modern American historian with a focus on religious and cultural history. Dr. Connelly teaches survey courses on the history of the United States, a class on Historical Methods for History majors, and upper level courses on topics like the New South, the Civil Rights Movement, and Religion and American Culture. His current research and writing project focuses on the historical vision of Walker Percy.

Dr. Timothy Fritz is an Associate Professor and Department Chair of History at Mount St. Mary's University. He teaches classes on pirates, comparative slave rebellions, the American Revolution, civil rights, and other topics in American history. Dr. Fritz is a historian of race and early America and has published articles in the *South Carolina Historical Magazine* and the *Journal of Social History*. He also directs the Parker-Dailey Seminar for Racial Reconciliation at Mount St. Mary's, leading students and faculty through sites of lament around the country.

Dr. Alicia K. Jackson is Associate Professor of African-American history at Covenant College. She received a 2016 Louisville Project Grant, which she used to study the life and work of Isaac Anderson, a black minister and politician who lived during Reconstruction. Dr. Jackson's book on Anderson, The Recovered Life of Isaac Anderson, was released in November of 2021. Her new project focuses on southern Appalachia and examines the lives of Black communities in northwest Georgia and southeast Tennessee.

Dr. Karen Johnson is a historian of race and religion in the twentieth century United States. Her first book, *One in Christ: Chicago Catholics and the Quest for Interracial Justice* (Oxford, 2018) used Catholic interracial activism as a lens to explore the role of religion in civil rights in the North. Her co-edited book *Understanding and Teaching Religion in US History* (University of Wisconsin Press, forthcoming 2023) brings recent historiography into teachers' hands and offers concrete ways to incorporate religious history into their classrooms. Her current book project uses case studies to explore how thinking Christianly and historically about race's effects on American worship might help churches foster reconciliation and justice in the present.

Gregory R. Perry served 14 years as Associate Professor of New Testament and the Director of the City Ministry Initiative at Covenant Seminary in St Louis. He currently serves as the Vice President of Strategic Projects for Third Millennium Ministries in Orlando. He is the author of The Drama of Discipleship, published in 2022 by Cascade Books, an imprint of Wipf and Stock.

Dr. Otis W. Pickett is University Historian at Clemson University. Pickett has articles published in the *Journal of African American History*, the *Native South*, the *Southern Quarterly*, the *Journal of the South Carolina Historical Association* and has contributed book chapters for several books including *Southern Religion, Southern Culture: Essays Honoring Charles Reagan Wilson* (University Press of Mississippi, 2018). Dr. Pickett also taught courses at Parchman Penitentiary and Central Mississippi Correctional Facility through the Prison to College Pipeline Program, which he and Dr. Patrick Alexander co-founded in 2013. Pickett, Alexander and the PTCPP teaching team were awarded Educator of the Year from the Mississippi Humanities Council in 2018.

Dr. Trisha Posey is Professor of history and director of the Honors Scholars Program at John Brown University. Her primary academic interest is the relationship between religion and reform in the 19th-century United States. She has also studied the history of slavery in the United States as well as the enduring legacy of racism left by slavery. Her other areas of academic interest include African history, the history of poverty and welfare, and genocide. She has published numerous articles and book chapters on American religion and reform, teaching about genocide, and the history of Christian higher education in Africa.

Dr. Ansley Quiros is Associate Professor of history at the University of North Alabama. She is a historian of the twentieth century United States, with a focus on race, politics, and religion. Her first book, *God With Us: Lived Theology and the Black Freedom Struggle in Americus, Georgia, 1942–1976* (UNC, 2018) examines the struggle over race and Christian theology in

Southwest Georgia. She is currently working on a biography of Charles and Shirley Sherrod.

Dr. Peter Slade is Professor of the history of Christianity and Christian thought at Ashland University. Slade's first book, *Open Friendship in a Closed Society: Mission Mississippi and a Theology of Friendship* (Oxford University Press, 2009), is an interdisciplinary study of an ecumenical racial reconciliation initiative in Mississippi. He has been a coeditor of and contributor to three volumes with the Project on Lived Theology: *Lived Theology: New Perspectives on Method, Style, and Pedagogy* (Oxford University Press, 2016); *Mobilizing for the Common Good: The Lived Theology of John M. Perkins* (University Press of Mississippi, 2013); and *People Get Ready: Thirteen Jesus-Haunted Misfits, Malcontents and Dreamers for Troubled Times* (Eerdmans, 2022).